Core Christianity

The Tie That Binds

—ɱ—

Charles J. Colton

Core Christianity: The Tie That Binds
by Charles J. Colton

Printed in the United States of America

ISBN 1-60034-349-X

www.xulonpress.com

Dedication

—ᗰᗰ—

By the grace of God, this work is done. It is dedicated foremost to my family—my mom and dad, James and Hideko Colton, who took me to a church that preached the biblical Gospel; Lisabeth, my loving wife of twenty years, who has never known me except as one still in school; my three above-average children James, Samuel, and Anne, whose dad was frequently off somewhere studying; and my elder brother Dr. Carl G. Colton, who has always been a tough act to follow.

I wish to acknowledge, as well, Rev. W. Robert Mattox and Rev. Thomas G. Kesinger, whose teaching and godly example greatly influenced me to pursue vocational ministry; and Dr. John H. Mulholland, Dr. James R. Mook, and Dr. Thomas R. Edgar of Capital Bible Seminary, whose courses challenged as well as blessed me over many memorable years while my family lived, worked, and went to school in Virginia.

I wish to express my thanks to Dr. Howard Bixby, Dr. James King, and Dr. Michael D. Stallard of Baptist Bible Seminary, all of whom endured more than their fair share of impertinence as I completed the D.Min. program over way too many years. I am especially grateful to Dr. Stallard for his respectful guidance on the dissertation project which serves as the basis of this book. What shortcomings that remain are entirely my own.

I am indebted, as well, to the good people of the Panama Baptist Church, New York, who suffered (?) my absence while away at seminary, endured my preoccupation with school work while at home, and underwrote a significant portion of my education. I am particularly grateful to Rev. Andy Cook, Associate Pastor of Youth and Life Ministries, for his collaboration on the Pastoral Policy on Christian Cooperation presented in Chapter 8. Finally, I wish to thank the people of Paw Paw Bible Church, West Virginia, for over five memorable years of ministry together, and for our joint work on the Statement of Faith shown in Chapter 9.

It is with a great deal of uneasiness that I have tried to single out individual persons for their contributions to my life and ministry generally, and to this project in particular. I profoundly regret any notable omissions, should there be any. If you are one of them and would trouble yourself to look me up, I would gladly take you to lunch at a fine fast-food establishment.

Contents

—m—

1	Introduction	11

Figuring Out the Core **23**

2	The Historic Creeds and Core Christianity, Part 1	25
3	The Historic Creeds and Core Christianity, Part 2	37
4	Modern Challenges to Core Christianity	51
5	The New Testament Witness to Core Christianity	63

Living Out the Core **83**

6	Application to Inter-Church Ministry, Part 1	85
7	Application to Inter-Church Ministry, Part 2	97
8	A Practical Guide to Cooperative Ministry	111
9	Application to Intra-Church Ministry	123
10	The Importance of Continued Indoctrination	137

11   The Power to Change................................151

12   Conclusion 165

Appendix A 173

Appendix B 187

Bibliography 211

How To Become a Christian 217

List Of Tables and Figures

The Fundamentalist View of the Western Christian World............19

Summary of Views Concerning Essential Evangelicalism............60

Summary of the Apostolic Message In Acts.................................75

Churches In the GARBC 92

The Circumference Defining the Center.......................................143

Labels and Descriptors That Characterize Change.....................162

The Prophetic Decision Tree...181

Cover Letter to the GARBC Council Of Eighteen 189

Letter to the Empire State Fellowship 190

Chapter 1

Introduction

—ᴍᴍ—

Pastor James was in quite the quandary. The rural community in which he had lived and ministered for less than a year had asked him to participate in a joint prayer service following the vicious September 11th terrorist attack on the World Trade Center towers in New York City. Although that event was hundreds of miles distant, still the shock and horror of what had happened to so many innocent victims had reached directly into his small hamlet and began to sow feelings of intense anger, frustration, and grief in most everyone he knew. People searched for answers. There grew a natural desire to draw the community together in a time of unprecedented confusion. Pastor James himself desired to minister to his friends and neighbors in a big way.

The only other minister planning to participate in the prayer service was the pastor of the church just down the road from his own independent church. While the other church was a theologically conservative congregation with a strong, biblical ministry in the community, it was affiliated with a large mainline denomination well-known for its theological inclusiveness and, at least in some quarters, its permissive attitude toward individuals involved in open immorality. In fact, some persons in the denomination continued to serve in positions of authority even as they openly persisted in behavior that might be characterized as, among other things, perverse and against the very nature of things.

A number of unconnected thoughts began to swirl around in Pastor James' mind and vie for attention—the biblical focus and explicit Gospel witness of the mainline pastor, the cordial personal and professional relationship he had developed with him, the outright apostasy and moral indifference that existed elsewhere in that pastor's wide-ranging denomination, his own personal reputation in the small community in which he served, his desire to have a meaningful presence there.

Then there was the issue of denominational distinctiveness. Apart from the conservative/liberal split in his colleague's denomination, there were the things that always distinguished "us" and "them"—the proper mode of baptism, eternal security, certain practical aspects of sanctification.[1] Pastor James had always been taught that the sure-fire way to remain separate and distinct in doctrine was to minister in separate and distinct spheres. To preserve one's doctrinal heritage meant that one had to position himself as far away from other theological camps as one could manage. Doctrinal integrity was completely bound up with the integrity of the imagined perimeter fences that generations of faithful followers had established around his church, not unlike the chain link and barbwire fences that ringed the many secretive installations which Pastor James used to visit in his former life as a Government contractor. Those faithful followers just knew that doctrinal compromise and eventual defeat would come by enemy infiltration from the outside rather than from agitation on the inside. As Pastor James mused over these things, he began to reflect upon the way that terrorists had infiltrated America's cities and suburbs over the course of several years before turning their sights on the World Trade Center.

In the end, Pastor James could not make up his mind. He *felt* that he ought to participate, but he knew better than to act on his ill-defined feelings. And besides, there was simply too much at risk in going ahead. He knew that if he agreed to co-sponsor the community prayer service, his colleagues in the sister churches of his own ecclesiastical association would react adversely, and perhaps even begin to censor him or withdraw their fellowship. Pastor James decided in the end to play it safe this time around. He reached for the phone to let the prayer service organizers know of his decision. It would not be an easy call to make. At the same time, he resolved to devote a sizeable portion of his time over the next few years to research the extent to which separating from other Christians was really necessary, a practice he had been taught over many years in the churches with which he had affiliated. Next time, he thought to himself, he would at least be prepared to follow his own hard-won convictions, and sound a clear note when asked to respond to another opportunity for cooperative ministry.

While this story is fictitious, several of its more prominent features will undoubtedly resonate with many of the pastors, church leaders, and laypersons who read this book. Unless one's ministry is predominantly to mainline churches, these are the issues with which a believer is confronted when working within the framework of an historically fundamentalist ministry. Anyone who approaches too closely to the perimeter fence, except to mend it or build it higher, is viewed with suspicion. To step outside the fence and mix with Christians from another tradition is to invite outright hostility.

Before delving into some of the issues that plagued Pastor James, let it be said that his central concern about doctrinal purity is biblically well-founded. Whatever church we choose to identify with, we need to be sure of what we believe, and then pass the torch of that belief to succeeding generations. While not everyone can possibly be "right" on a matter of doctrine for which there are diametrically opposed viewpoints,[2] still each of us must at least be faithful to what we believe the Bible is saying. We ought at least to be convinced of the things that we teach and practice. As a practical matter, conformity to the doctrine and practice of a church is largely the basis of unity within that body. Virtually without exception, the more inclusive mainline denominations are being torn apart today, not by forces outside their ranks, but by theological schismatics within their own ranks—those who refuse to conform to the declared beliefs and behavioral standards of their churches.

As the pastor of an independent church, Pastor James may rightly have sensed as well that, while doctrine had always been what defined and differentiated various church traditions, it served a more central if not *critical* role in the church in which he ministered. Older, established churches that are independent did not usually start out that way. In other words, they made a decision at some point in their history to break away from the larger body of churches to which they belonged. Often that decision was made because the larger group had relaxed its commitment to a biblical standard of truth either in teaching or in practice, at least with any measure of consistency. To be true to itself, then, the independent church is always having to justify its continued detachment, whether consciously or not. In other words, being independent, that church must decide for itself, through its shared understanding of Scripture, what is so distinctive about its beliefs that it must remain aloof from the larger body of churches whence it came, or, for that matter, from the churches of another tradition altogether.

If in that ongoing analysis it becomes apparent that nothing of substance can any longer be identified and upheld as distinctive, then that church's need to exist as an independent organization becomes open to question. We may look at it this way—if a church is defined primarily by its doctrine, and historically at least that has been true, then without a set of enduring doctrinal distinctives, an independent church may as well affiliate once more with any number of inclusive denominations—those which pay hardly more than lip service (at best, scarce attention) to any abiding standard or test of Christian orthodoxy. Any church that has separated itself from the wider body ought always to ask a series of questions. Why are we independent? What, if anything, has changed in the parent denomination since our church chose to disassociate? How have we changed since then?

Adding to Pastor James' concern was the very fact that his church was not only independent, it was conservative and *evangelical*. As an evangelical church, it would have professed allegiance to the Bible as God's fully trustworthy record and revelation of Himself to Man, as an authoritative measure of what is actually true. Such convictions require that a church place greater stress on the cognitive (knowable) content of its doctrine than those churches, say, within the more neo-orthodox or liberal strands of Christianity, for which the Bible is considered to be the mere record of man's quest for God, rather than the written Word of God that it is. This emphasis upon holding to the truth of God's Word is important to any evangelical congregation, whether or not it is independent.

There was an opposite battle brewing in Pastor James' mind. Certainly it is important to consider the implications of being either denominational or independent, just as it is critical to ask whether one's church is theologically conservative or liberal. But somewhere along the way it seems that it is equally important to place some limits on all the labeling. To qualify as a liberal, did one have to deny the deity of Christ, or could one merely question the extent of the biblical flood? Beneath questions such as this lies the bigger question: Cannot one distinguish what is *distinctive* about a particular church's teaching from what is *essential* to its being Christian and in any sense biblical, and on *that* basis forge a relationship? Pastor James seemed to have begun to consider this question, even if he could not articulate what caused him to feel as he did. For all the theological and methodological differences that existed between the two churches in his community, there still were more than a few core beliefs that drew the churches together.

Unless one is prepared to admit no other church body as Christian except one's own, this reality would appear to be self-evident. Belief in a pretribulational Rapture,[3] for example, is not a requirement for taking the Christian label. Nor is commitment to a congregational form of church government necessary to Christian identity.[4] Likewise, at the other extreme, it is apparent that some minimal set of essential beliefs must be affirmed before the Christian label begins to apply at all. In other words, mere assent to the existence of God, however that may be defined, does not make one a Christian. One may be a theist or a deist, even a pantheist, without ever becoming a Christian.[5] Antony Flew, one of the most significant philosophers of our day, and until recently the world's most famous atheist, now believes in God. Still, he is not a Christian, nor would he profess to be. Nor does assent to a set of "Christian" principles or morals make one Christian, for Christianity is much more than some vaguely perceived code of personal behavior.

The first extreme is the error of certain strident forms of fundamentalism. Within these circles,[6] the western Christian church and its history looks something like that shown in Figure 1. Everything is rather cut-and-dried—churches are categorized and appropriately characterized as being either fundamental, compromising (new evangelical), liberal, or Catholic. The new evangelical and liberal are represented in Figure 1 by their umbrella organizations, the National Association of Evangelicals (NAE),[7] and National and World Council of Churches (WCC), respectively.

While these representations are a gross generalization of a much more complex religious landscape, they fairly well represent what the strident fundamentalist sees when looking through his viewfinder. As he sees it, there exists a great divide between fundamentalism and everyone else, the existence of which is clearly understood by anyone who takes his Bible seriously, for one is uncompromisingly biblical in degree as one is separated from the "compromisers." That is the error of strident fundamentalism. Those within this camp build elaborate perimeter fences to keep others away and, as importantly, to hold close and protect those who are on the inside. Beyond that fence, the larger church scene is a dangerous place, indeed.

Conversely, the failure to define and uphold at least a minimum set of essential beliefs is the error of theological relativism or liberalism. Most mainline denominations subscribe to a rather liberal or *inclusivist* membership policy, which is another way of saying that one's particular theology is welcome so long as one supports the programs of the church financially. In this paradigm for inter-church ministry, any notion of separation is dismissed altogether as divisive and unloving. What binds the mainline denomination together is purely organizational or, at best, missional and methodological, but never is it theological. While lip service is paid to some historical, usually orthodox Christian creed, what is actually believed by clergy and laity is quite divergent.

So what are we to make of all these different approaches to handling "truth"? Who is right? Who is "off the deep end"? Should a distinction be made between what is essential and what is distinctive to one's Christian faith? On these questions, both the fundamentalist and the liberal accuse the other of being well outside the mainstream. For the liberal, "mainstream" has to do with what the majority of churches are teaching and doing. For the fundamentalist, "mainstream" has to do with what the churches have historically

Figure 1. The Fundamentalist View of the
Western Christian World.

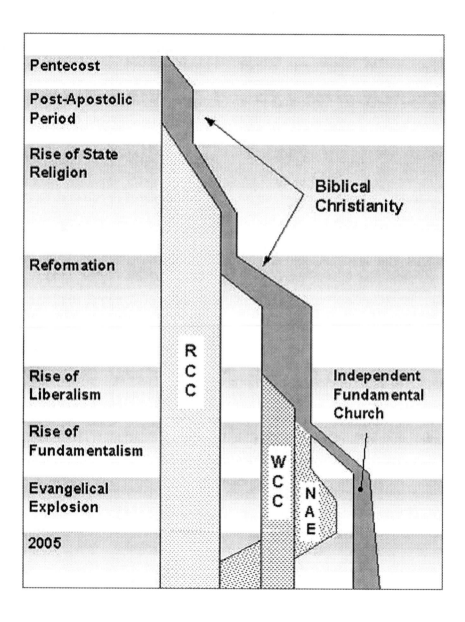

stood for. The fundamentalist views himself as standing directly in the stream of biblical, apostolic teaching.

The thesis of this book is that the "truth" lies somewhere between the strident fundamentalist and the inclusive liberal. We will set out to demonstrate that there is a set of core values or beliefs that provide necessary cohesion among Christian churches, but that many other values and beliefs, while distinctive to a particular denomination — or congregation in the case of an independent church — should not be part of any test of fellowship or cooperation. While that thesis may already be tacitly assumed by many evangelical Christians, still it must be proven by Scripture. Neither the fundamentalist nor the liberal is free to stand on presumption.

What may not be so clear to evangelical Christians — even among those who would give *a priori* approval to the thesis — is how that attitude should affect, even guide, a church's practice, or philosophy of ministry. In other words, certain practical ramifications may fall out of an acceptance of the primary thesis. Many self-identified fundamentalists, for example, would gladly affirm that church groups outside their own may claim and use the Christian name. Their strong distaste for "compromise" nonetheless leads them to a strict practice of separatism, even from among those who agree with them upon the essentials.[8] Is this practice evidence of strong biblical principle, or is it (perhaps) evidence instead of gross spiritual arrogance? Mark Noll has written, "To confuse the distinctive with the essential is to compromise the life-transforming character of the Christian faith."[9] If he is right in what he says, then far too many fundamentalists have compromised upon what is central to Christian belief.[10]

The major purpose of this book, then, is two-fold. The first is to attempt a definition of what is *essential* or *core* Christianity. That is, given the often wide variation in beliefs that exist even among self-confessing evangelical church groups and individuals, is there at least a core set of beliefs for which one may rightly be called *evangelical*, even if disagreement remains on everything else? We must settle on a core set of beliefs lest the remainder of the book become hopelessly theoretical and thus devoid of any practicality.

That brings us to our second major purpose, which is to draw some practical applications of that understanding to independent intra- and inter-church life. *Intra*-church life has to do with how a church conducts its own internal affairs. A church may use its doctrinal standards as a test of fellowship (i.e., membership), or as a rule by which potential teachers are measured for suitability. *Inter*-church life has more to do with how a church relates to the Christian world outside. If two churches agree upon what is essential even while they differ over certain non-essentials, perhaps there is something biblical about their getting on with a visible demonstration of unity under the Lordship of Christ.

Discussion Questions

1. To what denomination or association(s) does your church belong? If your church does not belong to any denomination or association, why not? You may want to speak with your pastor or church leader for help with your answer.

2. List two or more beliefs held by your church that make it what it is (e.g., Baptist, Methodist, Pentecostal, etc.), giving biblical support if possible. Again, ask a church leader if you need assistance.

3. What beliefs does your church hold that are essential to its being Christian? Do other area churches share those same beliefs? You may want to consult with Christian friends outside your church.

4. To what degree does your church presently cooperate with other churches in your area? How does your church decide with whom it may work together?

5. How important is visible Christian unity to the witness of Christ in your community? How might disunity affect a non-Christian's decision to make a first-time commitment to Christ?

Part One

Figuring Out the Core

—ᴍ—

Chapter 2

The Historic Creeds and Core Christianity, Part 1

—ɯ—

—∿—

In this chapter and the next, we trace some attempts to define "essential" or "core" Christianity as witnessed in the earlier, catholic[1] writings of the Church, as well as in the much later Protestant creeds. This investigation will serve as a first step toward developing an understanding of what "essential" actually means. What drives this investigation is a tentative acceptance of the statement made at the end of the last chapter—If various churches can agree upon what is essential even while they differ over certain non-essentials, perhaps there is something biblical about their getting on with a visible demonstration of unity under the Lordship of Christ. Before we are finished, we will need to prove that supposition, but for now it serves as pretext for pressing ahead with our investigation.

We must look at the ancient sources referenced above for the simple reason that any determination of what is essential to Christianity ought to be historically informed, given that Christianity claims for itself to be rooted ultimately in the revelation of God in and through history. Evangelicalism,[2] at least as it has been popularized, is notorious for its lack of historical perspective on a wide range of issues. In fact, while it is claimed that evangelical faith

> If various churches can agree upon what is essential even while they differ over certain non-essentials, perhaps there is something biblical about their getting on with a visible demonstration of unity under the Lordship of Christ.

is based exclusively in Scripture, it is equally rooted in the early catholic faith of the Church Fathers, as well as in the later (and more sectarian) Protestant creeds. In Chapter 4, we will take up the question of what is essential to Christian faith as depicted in the writings of early twentieth century fundamentalists and the later evangelicals. A review and analysis of scriptural passages that help to clarify the substance of core Christian faith is reserved for Chapter 5.

Early attempts at definition

Many of our core evangelical doctrinal commitments find their expression in the doctrinal affirmations of the earliest Christian polemicists, as a brief summary of two of the most well-known creeds will demonstrate. Early post-apostolic Christians were required to codify their core beliefs in creeds, in response to challenges by both pagans outside the Church and heretics within. In this way, they established a clear confession of essential belief that could be used to discriminate what was orthodox from what was heterodox. Of the many creeds that survive to the present day, the two most well-known are the Apostles' Creed and the Nicene Creed.

Apostles' Creed. Of these two historic creeds, the Apostles' Creed is perhaps the more widely received among the Protestant churches. Of course, any creed will emphasize the beliefs that stand opposite those errors which are prevalent at the time of writing. The Apostles' Creed is no exception to this rule; drawn up in the first or second century, it emphasizes the true humanity and real body of Jesus, answering to the Gnostic and Marcionite heretics of its own day:[3]

> I believe in God the Father Almighty, Maker of Heaven and Earth: And in Jesus Christ, His only Son, Our Lord; who was conceived by the Holy Ghost, born of the Virgin Mary, suffered under Pontius Pilate, was crucified, dead, and buried; He descended into Hades; the third day he rose again from the dead; He ascended into heaven, and sitteth on the right hand of

God, the Father Almighty; from thence he shall come
to judge the living and the dead. I believe in the Holy
Ghost, the holy catholic church, the communion of
saints, the forgiveness of sins, the resurrection of the
body, and the life everlasting. Amen.

Even allowing for a degree of historical conditioning, it can
be readily observed that the Apostles' Creed is still comprised in
large measure of several basic tenets of the Christian faith, which
together summarize that faith as to its essential content. In particular, the Creed witnesses to an early, though perhaps incomplete,
Trinitarian understanding of God, bearing special testimony as it
does to the Father, Son, and Holy Spirit. And yet it gives special
place to the Lord Jesus Christ, affirming first His unique relationship
to the Father, and then His relationship to believers as their Lord.
Once having established the Person of Christ, it then affirms the
real historical and salvific work of Christ, namely, His death, burial,
resurrection, ascension, and second coming. Finally, through appeal
to a variety of biblical themes (e.g., forgiveness of sins, resurrection,
and eternal life), the Creed affirms a general belief in salvation. All
that is really missing from the Apostles' Creed that would especially
have endeared it to modern evangelicals is an explicit declaration
that justification[4] comes by faith alone. Given that this central theme
of Paul's appears to have been largely lost to the Church soon after
the apostolic age, it comes as no surprise to find it missing here.

Nicene Creed. If the Apostles' Creed was emphatic in affirming
the true humanity and real body of Jesus, then the Nicene Creed,
drawn up in the fourth century, is equally emphatic in the way that
it beautifully affirms the Deity of Christ, since it is directed against
the Arians who denied that Christ was fully God.

I believe in one God, the Father Almighty, maker of
heaven and earth, and of all things visible and invis-
ible; And in one Lord Jesus Christ, the only begotten
Son of God, begotten of his Father before all worlds,
God of God, Light of Light, very God of very God,

begotten, not made, being of one substance with the Father; by whom all things were made; who for us men and for our salvation came down from heaven, and was incarnate by the Holy Ghost of the Virgin Mary, and was made man; and was crucified also for us under Pontius Pilate; he suffered and was buried; and the third day he rose again according to the Scriptures, and ascended into heaven, and sitteth on the right hand of the Father; and he shall come again, with glory, to judge both the quick and the dead; whose kingdom shall have no end. And I believe in the Holy Ghost the Lord, and Giver of Live, who proceedeth from the Father and the Son; who with the Father and the Son together is worshipped and glorified; who spake by the Prophets. And I believe one holy catholic and apostolic Church; I acknowledge one baptism for the remission of sins; and I look for the resurrection of the dead, and the life of the world to come. Amen.

This creed contains much in common with the Apostles' Creed, but adds concerning Christ that He is "God of God, Light of Light, very God of very God, begotten, not made, being of one substance with the Father; by whom all things were made. . . ."[5] Furthermore, an explicit witness to the Trinity is given by the following on the Holy Spirit: "And I believe in the Holy Ghost the Lord, and Giver of Life, who proceedeth from the Father and the Son;[6] who with the Father and the Son together is worshipped and glorified. . . ." Again, despite their respective emphases, both creeds stress the Person of Christ and His real, historical death, burial, resurrection, ascension, and second coming. Furthermore, both creeds affirm a general belief in salvation. The Nicene deals with the manner in which that salvation is appropriated—namely, by "baptism for the remission of sins." That understanding is best viewed as a disappointing reflection of the sacramental theology[7] that had already infiltrated the Church by that time.

The Protestant creeds

The Protestant movement began picking up steam when certain reform-minded thinkers drew attention to a continuing and long-standing departure by Roman Catholic clergy away from biblical standards of faith. The Protestant Reformation is best viewed as an attempt on the part of these reformers to restore biblical practice to the Western Church—for the most part these reformers were not separatist in their thinking, at least initially. Rome's summary denunciation of their concerns and the expulsion of key leaders such as Martin Luther, however, eventually sparked a wide-spread exodus from the Church as a tactical matter. The year that the Protestant Reformation started is commonly accepted as 1517, when Luther posted his now-famous Ninety-Five Theses upon the church door at Wittenberg, Germany.[8] Luther's Theses actually amounted to no more than a challenge for scholarly debate on the Catholic practice of dispensing indulgences.[9] It was left to Philip Melanchthon to write the *Augsburg Confession*, which contains the essence of historic Lutheran belief.

Around the same period, a priest by the name of Ulrich Zwingli began a reform movement at Zurich, Switzerland, having come into contact with Luther's ideas. John Calvin would initiate a parallel reform movement at Geneva. Together, these men are credited with launching what would come to be known as the Reformed faith. Reformed ideas quickly took root in the English church under Protestant Archbishop of Canterbury Thomas Cranmer. For almost three subsequent decades under four successive monarchs, the English church wavered between Reformed Protestantism and Catholicism. Under Queen Elizabeth I, the Church of England adopted a "Via Media," settling for Catholic ritual but Reformed doctrine. That doctrine is represented in *The Thirty-Nine Articles*.[10]

Taken together, Lutheranism, the Reformed Movement, the English Reformation, and their derivatives comprised the so-called Magisterial Reformation. Each of these movements, like the Roman Catholic Church that preceded them, was dependent upon sanction by the state. The so-called Radical Reformation, by contrast, sought to follow even more faithfully the biblical-apostolic model, in part by renouncing any connection between state and church. Without protective cover, Radical Reformers such as the Anabaptists found themselves under persecution by both Catholics and Protestants. Anabaptism is perhaps best represented today in the Mennonite movement, but its theological influence is seen in the development of the various Baptist movements, as well. The Baptist churches in America grew largely out of the English Baptist movement, itself an offshoot of the English Reformation through the Puritans. Historic Baptist convictions in America are represented in *The New Hampshire Confession of Faith.*

The Thirty-Nine Articles. In the remainder of this chapter, we start by taking up *The Thirty-Nine Articles* of the Church of England as representative of the views historically held by Reformed Protestantism. As we continue giving attention to the doctrinal standards of the various Protestant churches, we will begin to see how agreed the various Protestant sectarian creeds really are, containing both the *essence* of biblical and apostolic Christian faith, along with those beliefs which are distinctive of a particular faith tradition. We may summarize the Anglican creed as follows:

I-V   Affirms that in the "unity of [the] Godhead there be three persons, of one substance, power, and eternity; the Father, the Son, and the Holy Ghost." Clearly presents both the divine and human natures in Christ, as well as the full scope of His salvific work, including His sacrificial death for our sins, His decent into Hell, His bodily resurrection, and His ascension to heaven.

VI-VIII   Deals with the sufficiency of Scripture for salvation; the question of canonicity; the relation of the Old Testament to the New; the ceremonial, civil, and moral aspects of the Law, the latter declared to be binding upon the Christian; and the reliability of the Nicene and Apostles' Creed as based in Scripture.

IX-XVIII   Covers several aspects of salvation, including the fact of original sin (and continuing sin in the believer), the extent of free will, the nature of justification, the necessity of faith, the place of good works, the sinlessness of Christ, and the purpose of God in predestination and election.

XIX-XXXVI

Defines the visible Church as "a congregation of faithful men in which the pure Word of God is preached, and the Sacraments duly administered." Argues for the necessity and inherent authority of duly ordained ministers, upholds the authority of the Church so long as its decrees are in accordance with Scripture, gives careful attention to both the meaning and mode of Baptism and the Lord's Supper, and affords the possibility of excommunication, all the while denouncing Catholic heresies.

XXXVII-XXXIX

Acknowledges the legitimacy and authority of civil authority except in spiritual matters. Allows that a Christian may serve in the armed forces and swear before a magistrate when required to do so. Upholds the notion of personal property, and yet enjoining Christians to share liberally with those in need.

These latter three articles deal with the relationship of churchmen to the government. Articles XIX-XXXVI, besides holding forth an Anglican view of the Church, its ministers, and its sacraments, contain a rich polemic against some of the more unscriptural beliefs and practices among Catholics, such as purgatory[11], transubstantiation[12], the sacrifice of the mass, and enforced celibacy of the priesthood. Thus, it is in what remains, Articles I-XVIII, that we can hope to find what, according to the Anglicans, is essential to Christian faith.

As has been pointed out, Articles I-V affirm the Trinity, the full deity and humanity of Jesus, His sacrificial death for our sins, bodily resurrection, and ascension to heaven.[13] A short description of the Holy Spirit, including His procession from both the Father and the Son, is provided, as well. Following a treatment of the sufficiency and unity of Scripture in Articles VI-VIII, which we may treat parenthetically as the basis of all that follows,[14] *The Thirty-Nine Articles* picks up with the need of salvation in that "man is very far gone from original righteousness," and the means of salvation—namely that "we are accounted righteous before God only for the merit of our Lord and Savior Jesus Christ, by faith, and not for our own works or deservings." Next it includes, "Wherefore . . . we are justified by faith, only." What is clear in the Anglican understanding of salvation is that we are justified by faith alone on account of Christ's righteousness and not on account of our good works. While salvation begins with God's gracious purpose in predestination and election, it ends in faith as men obey the Gospel.

To summarize, setting aside some very necessary statements about the Bible, *The Thirty-Nine Articles* deal directly with salvation in a thoroughgoing, evangelical spirit—why Christ in His Person is uniquely qualified to offer it, what Christ did by His death, resurrection, (descent into Hell) and ascension to provide for it, our real need of it, and what we must do by way of faith to receive it. Risking a bit of reductionism, *The Thirty-Nine Articles* deal in who Christ is, what He did to save us, and what we must do to be saved. Only then did the Church of England proceed to distinguish itself ecclesiastically and in relationship to civil authority. Between matters of scriptural authority and ecclesiastical posturing, at the core there is the basis in doctrine of a hearty, Bible-based, evangelical faith.

The Thirty-Nine Articles comprise just the first of several Protestant creeds with which we will interact in the next chapter. At its core, it explains the central teachings of the Protestant churches in the Reformed tradition on matters related to the person of Christ, His saving work, and the means by which that work may be appropriated unto salvation. What proves quite remarkable is the way that other Protestant traditions will deviate from *The Thirty-Nine Articles* around the edges, even to a fair degree, but will faithfully preserve that which we have discovered at the core.

Discussion Questions

1. According to the author, what key belief is missing from the Apostles' Creed that would have given it much wider appeal among modern-day evangelicals?

2. Again, in the author's view, why does the Nicene Creed teach that sins are remitted through baptism? Upon what basis may evangelicals contest that view today?

3. Compare the ancient creeds and *The Thirty-Nine Articles*. At what points do they agree? Where do they differ?

4. According to the Church of England, what is the sole response to the message concerning Christ that is necessary for salvation? How does that understanding of salvation compare with the teaching in your church?

5. As one whose church affiliation is likely other than Anglican or Episcopal, were you surprised by the similarity of their stated belief as compared to your own? What may help to explain the similarity?

Chapter 3

The Historic Creeds and Core Christianity, Part 2

The review of *The Thirty-Nine Articles* in the last chapter serves as a basis of comparison for other creedal documents. In this chapter, we continue our look at Protestant creeds first by taking up the *New Hampshire Confession* as representative of Baptist belief. We will see that the *New Hampshire Confession* contains the major doctrines set forth by the Reformed tradition, as well as added Anabaptist distinctives. For good measure, we then take up a brief analysis of the *Articles of Religion of the Methodist Church* as broadly representative of Methodist belief, again containing major Reformed themes but with revisions and additions that reflect certain Wesleyan distinctives. To complete our survey of the various Protestant faith statements, we close by touching briefly on the *Augsburg Confession*, as representative of Lutheran belief. Throughout this discussion, we will make comparative reference to *The Thirty-Nine Articles*. By giving attention to these documents, we will see how agreed the various Protestant sectarian creeds really are, containing both the *essence* of biblical and apostolic Christian faith, along with those beliefs which are distinctive of a particular faith tradition.

New Hampshire Confession.[1] The *New Hampshire Confession* dates back to 1830, when a faith statement was prepared for use by Baptists in that state. Minor revisions were made in 1890, and since then the creed has enjoyed wide circulation among Baptists in America. The creed contains twenty articles dealing with various points of doctrine. While the *New Hampshire Confession* bears all the marks of being a sectarian creed (containing, as it does, numerous theological tenets that are distinctive to Baptists), still it is not difficult to isolate what is essential from what is distinctive. We may summarize the creed as follows:[2]

The Bible

I. *The Scriptures.* Emphasizing its divine inspiration and authority, having "salvation for its end, and truth without any mixture of error for its matter."

God

II. *The True God.* Revealing a Trinitarian understanding of the one God, and expressing several of His attributes.

Salvation

III. *The Fall of Man.* Describing the origin and nature of sin, such that mankind stands in need of salvation.

IV. *God's Purpose of Grace.* Basing election in God's eternal and sovereign purpose, though it is effected through means of grace.

V. *The Way of Salvation.* Making Christ to be a uniquely qualified Savior by virtue of His divine and human nature, obedient life, atoning death, resurrection, and ascension.

VI. *Of Regeneration.* Defining the Holy Spirit's necessary role in salvation as the impartation of a new nature resulting in a new and holy disposition, being evidenced in a changed life.

VII. *Of Repentance.* Setting forth repentance as being a godly sorrow over sin, a hatred of sin, and a turning from sin.

VIII.   *Of Faith.* Establishing faith as "the medium through which Christ is received by the soul as its sacrifice and Savior . . . consisting mainly of belief and trust."

Additional Reformed Distinctives

IX.   *Of Justification.* Declaring how Christ's righteousness is freely imputed through faith in His blood, and "not in consideration of any works of righteousness."

X.   *Of Adoption.* Noting how God accepts us as members of His family, with all attendant rights, privileges, and promises.

XI.   *Of Sanctification.* Teaching that believers are made to be "partakers of His holiness" in a process carried out by the Holy Spirit through the means of the Word of God.

XII.   *The Perseverance of the Saints.* Teaching the eternal security of those who show by their endurance that they are truly regenerate.

XIII.   *The Law and the Gospel.* Describing the role of the Gospel in delivering men from their sinful nature and restoring them to "unfeigned obedience to the holy Law."

Baptist Distinctives

XIV.   *A Gospel Church.* Setting forth the visible Church as a congregation of baptized believers associated by covenant, observing the ordinances, and having as officers pastors and deacons.

XV.   *Christian Baptism.* Defining baptism to be immersion in water as emblematic of faith in the crucified, buried, and risen Savior, and of death to sin and resurrection to a new life.

XVI.   *The Lord's Supper.* Stressing the symbolic and commemorative nature of the bread and wine.

XVII.   *The Christian Sabbath.* Setting apart the first day of the week as devoted to religious exercise.

XVIII. *Civil Government.* Stressing that, while divinely appointed, governments "have no rights of control over, or interference with, religious matters."

Last Things

XIX.   *Righteous and Wicked.* Setting forth a radical distinction between the righteous and the wicked, now and for eternity.

XX.   *The World to Come.* Affirming the Second Coming, the resurrection of the dead, and the endless consignment of the wicked to hell and the righteous to heaven.

Hopefully, the subtitles we have added help to show how the structure and flow of the *New Hampshire Confession* points to an understanding of what is essential to Christian faith versus what is distinctive to Baptist faith. While a certain degree of overlap is necessary in any theological document such as this, it is telling how the Confession begins with a declaration of belief in the Bible, followed by an affirmation of orthodox Trinitarianism. Next are the articles that deal with salvation, including the uniqueness of Jesus as God and Savior, as well as His death and resurrection for our sins. True to the emphasis in Protestantism generally, the Confession deals with what salvation requires on the part of the sinner—namely, repentance from sin and faith toward (in) Christ. Beyond that, the Confession gives precise definition to such key biblical and Reformed salvation themes as Justification, Regeneration, Election, Sanctification, and Perseverance.[3] It proceeds to Articles that lay out what is distinctive to the Baptist heritage.[4] These are relegated to the latter section of the document, except that consideration of End Time events are given last, as is characteristic of most faith statements.

To summarize, once the *New Hampshire Confession* has gotten past a very necessary statement about the Bible, it deals directly with salvation—our real need of it, why Christ in His Person is uniquely qualified to offer it, what He did by His death, resurrection, and ascension to provide for it, and what we must do in repentance and faith to receive it. Risking a bit of reductionism, the Confession deals in who Christ is, what He did to save us, and what we must do to be saved. Only then did the Baptists proceed to distinguish themselves theologically (as moderately Reformed) and ecclesiastically (demonstrating Anabaptist influence).

The Articles of Religion of the Methodist Church.[5] We next treat the Methodist *Articles of Religion* for the simple reason that Methodism, like the Baptist movement in England and America, is equally rooted in the English Reformed movement. The Methodist *Articles of Religion* were issued by John Wesley in 1784, immediately upon formal recognition of American independence in 1783. The document was officially adopted by the Methodist Episcopal Church in American in 1808.[6] Naturally, Wesley had his own set of particular concerns which were conditioned by the time and place in which he lived, not to mention the political climate of his day. His work has much in common with the Anglican/Episcopal *Thirty-Nine Articles*, repeating much of it verbatim or with minor revision, and is therefore most noteworthy for what it leaves out. Perhaps signaling his absolute reliance upon Scripture, Wesley omits Article VIII with its references both to the Nicene and Apostles' Creed. Another significant omission is that of Article XVII, dealing at length both with Predestination and Election. Several other omitted articles dealt with subjects that are of a more ecclesial or esoteric nature, such as the calling of ministers (Article XXIII), their inherent efficacy (Article XXVI), and the shunning of excommunicates (Article XXXIII). Still other articles appear to be omitted for sake of efficiency or expediency.[7] In the end, *The Articles of Religion* contain just twenty-five articles which may be broken down, for sake of brevity, as follows:

I-IV   Affirms that in the "unity of [the] Godhead there are three persons, of one substance, power, and eternity — the Father, the Son, and the Holy Ghost." Clearly presents both the divine and human natures in Christ, as well as the full scope of His salvific work, including His sacrificial death for our sins, His bodily resurrection, and His ascension to heaven.

V-VI   Deals with the sufficiency of Scripture for salvation, the question of canonicity, the relation of the Old Testament to the New, and the ceremonial, civil, and moral aspects of the Law, the latter declared to be binding upon the Christian.

VI-XII   Covers several aspects of salvation, including the fact of original sin (and continuing sin in the believer), the extent of free will, the nature of justification, the necessity of faith, and the place of good works.

XIII-XXII   Defines the visible Church as "a congregation of faithful men in which the pure Word of God is preached, and the Sacraments duly administered." Gives careful attention to both the meaning and mode of Baptism and the Lord's Supper, all the while denouncing Catholic heresies.

XXIII-XXV   Acknowledges that civil authority is vested in the United States Government, and that a Christian may swear before a magistrate when required to do so. Upholds the notion of personal property, and yet enjoining Christians to share liberally with those in need.

    These latter three articles most obviously bear the impress of the political scene surrounding John Wesley. Articles XIII-XXII, besides addressing a Wesleyan view of the Church and its sacraments, contain a rich polemic against some of the more unscriptural beliefs and practices among Catholics, such as purgatory, transubstantiation, the sacrifice of the mass, and enforced celibacy of the priesthood. Thus, as was true with *The Thirty-Nine Articles* of the Church of England, it is in what remains (Articles I-XII) that we can hope to find what, according to John Wesley, is essential to Christian faith.

As has been pointed out, Articles I-IV affirm the Trinity, the full deity and humanity of Jesus, His sacrificial death for our sins, bodily resurrection, and ascension to heaven. Wesley omitted the Anglican article setting forth Christ's descent into Hell. A short description of the Holy Spirit, including His procession from both the Father and the Son, is provided, as well. Following his treatment of the sufficiency and unity of Scripture in Articles V-VI, which we may treat parenthetically as the basis of all that follows,[8] Wesley picks up with the need of salvation in that "man is very far gone from original righteousness," and the means of salvation—namely that "we are accounted righteous before God only for the merit of our Lord and Savior Jesus Christ, by faith, and not for our own works or deservings." Next he includes, "Wherefore . . . we are justified by faith, only."

Article VIII merits special mention, in that it deals briefly with the issue of free will, and at least in seed form contains the Wesleyan concept of prevenient grace, whereby God restores a degree of free-will such as to enable the sinner to believe the Gospel. It should be noted once again, however, that Wesley only repeats what the *Thirty-Nine Articles* already declare. What is clear in Wesley's understanding is that we are justified by faith alone on account of Christ's righteousness and not on account of our good works. In Article X, Wesley is careful to treat good works as being "the fruits of faith" which "cannot put away our sins."

To summarize, setting aside some very necessary statements about the Bible, the *Articles of Religion* deal directly with salvation in a thoroughgoing, evangelical spirit—why Christ in His Person is uniquely qualified to offer it, what Christ did by His death, resurrection, and ascension to provide for it, our real need of it, and what we must do by way of faith to receive it. Again risking a bit of reductionism, the *Articles of Religion* deal in who Christ is, what He did to save us, and what we must do to be saved. Only then did Wesley proceed to distinguish his movement ecclesiastically and in relationship to civil authority.

Like the Baptist *New Hampshire Confession*, the *Articles of Religion* delegate the more distinctive tenets of Methodism to the latter sections of the document. Statements on such things as the proper mode of baptism and the precise nature and operation of the Church cover distinctive views which, when believed, make one a Methodist. Statements related to the nature of Christ, His atoning work, and the way of salvation concern essential tenets which, when believed, make one a Christian. In these essential areas, the Methodist *Articles of Religion* are for all practical purposes in complete agreement with the Baptist *New Hampshire Confession*. Wesley's lack of discourse on God's elective purpose in salvation does not materially affect how one actually *appropriates* salvation—namely, by faith and wholly apart from good works.

Augsburg Confession.[9] The *Augsburg Confession*, consisting of twenty-eight articles, was presented at the Diet of Augsburg in 1530, and included in the Book of Concord as the basic Lutheran confession in 1580.[10] The first twenty-one articles present basic Lutheran beliefs. The last seven reject abuses in the Christian life. Drickamer summarizes the Confession this way:

> It teaches the Trinity; original sin as true sin that would condemn if not forgiven; the deity and humanity of Jesus; his sacrifice for all human sin; justification by grace through faith without our works; the gospel, baptism, and the Lord's Supper as actual tools of the Holy Spirit to create and sustain faith; [and] good works as a result, not a cause, of salvation, motivated by the good news that salvation has been earned for us by Christ. . . . The abuses corrected include various false ideas and practices in the Lord's Supper; clerical celibacy; the misuse of confession and absolution; the dietary laws of medieval Romanism; and the idea of a hierarchy in visible Christendom having divine authority in matters of conscience.[11]

While evangelicals within the Reformed and Free Church movements[12] are justifiably troubled by Luther's view of the sacraments, it must be emphasized that what is taught by Luther is not at all inconsistent with his faith-only view of justification. According to the *Augsburg Confession*, baptism and the Lord's Supper are able to create and sustain faith only in that they are regarded as "signs and testimonies of the will of God . . . instituted to awaken and confirm faith in those who use them."[13] As such, they are perceived as being a form or symbol of the Word of God through which He reveals Himself to man, thus engendering faith.[14] In this way, Luther successfully distanced himself from the Roman Catholic view that salvation is actually received directly through the sacraments, *ex opere operato*.

By way of summary, then, the *Augsburg Confession* continues what is now a familiar pattern. Once past a necessary affirmation of orthodox Trinitarianism, it deals directly with the matter of salvation—our real need of it, why Christ in His Person is uniquely qualified to offer it, what Christ did to provide for it, and what we must do by way of faith to receive it. Here, the Lutherans are clear that "men cannot be justified before God by their own strength, merits, or works, but are freely justified for Christ's sake, through faith, when they believe that they are received into favor, and that their sins are forgiven."[15] Again risking oversimplification, the *Augsburg Confession* deals in who Christ is, what He did to save us, and what we must do to be saved. Only then did Melanchthon proceed to distinguish the Lutheran movement ecclesiastically, and especially in relation to medieval Roman Catholicism.

> While there are plenty of distinctive doctrinal points that serve to *denominate* the Protestant fold, there are a handful of essential doctrines that bind them together in the broader stream of historic Protestantism.

What is clear from an analysis of several of the historic Protestant creeds is that there is ample evidence for an essential body of belief to which every major branch of the Protestant church officially subscribes. Furthermore, that body of belief accords with early post-apostolic teaching, as determined through a comparison with the early Christian creeds, except in its emphasis upon faith apart from works as the means to entering into salvation. Again, this may be seen more as a necessary corrective to the sacramentalism spreading within the post-apostolic church.[16]

Of course, the immense divide existing between conservative and liberal elements within those branches is a reminder of how unfaithful many churches have been to practice and defend those core beliefs. Nevertheless, at least among the conservatives within the various Protestant groups, there is essential agreement in belief and practice. While there are plenty of distinctive doctrinal points that serve to *denominate* the Protestant fold, there are a handful of essential doctrines that bind them together in the broader stream of historic Protestantism.

To be specific, when it comes to a proper identification of Jesus Christ, His complete and sacrificial work for our salvation by death and resurrection, and our necessary response to that completed work—namely, faith apart from a consideration of our works—evangelicals find broad agreement among themselves, and across virtually every denominational frontier. Indeed, the Protestant church looks less like a patchwork and more like a priceless quilt—each square a bit different, and yet each completing the whole.

Discussion Questions

1. Upon what historic doctrines do the various Protestant denominations agree? Is there sufficient agreement to justify (limited) cooperation? Why or why not?

2. At what points do the Protestant churches differ most significantly with Roman Catholic teaching? How might those differences discourage cooperation?

3. The Methodist *Articles of Religion* bear a striking resemblance to the Anglican *Thirty-Nine Articles*. Why is that the case? Do Methodists and Anglicans differ on essential doctrine? Why or why not?

4. Baptist and Methodist communities appear to be more distinct from Roman Catholicism than, say, Lutheran and Anglican/ Episcopal communities. Historically, why is that so? How might historical "distance" affect the ability of churches to work together today?

5. As you interact with people who affiliate with other Christian denominations, do they evidence a clear understanding of salvation? What about people who are connected with your own church?

Chapter 4

Modern Challenges to Core Christianity

—ɷ—

In this chapter we continue with our attempt to extract what is considered "essential" to Christian faith by examining the writings of early fundamentalists and later evangelicals in the twentieth century. The early reformers took their leave of the Roman Catholic Church when it became necessary to restore a clear witness to the saving Gospel. At best, this Gospel was veiled in the teaching and practice of the dominant church. In the late nineteenth and early twentieth centuries, evangelicals in America had to wage their own theological battles against those within the established Protestant churches who once more began to defect away from the biblical Gospel. As before, it became necessary to clearly define and defend what was absolutely essential to biblical Christian faith.

New battle lines were drawn when theological liberals thought to redefine what constituted essential Christianity in a misguided attempt to rescue Christian faith from its cultural enemies. Long-held doctrines concerning the person of Christ, the redemptive value of His death, and the reality of His physical resurrection were envisioned as merely the cultural, and thus temporary, symbols that pointed to a more general and timeless set of principles. According to the theological liberal, these principles comprised the true essence of Christian religion.[1]

Early Fundamentalists

As theological liberalism increasingly gained a foothold in denominational schools and churches, the early fundamentalists began their own counter-offensive. They correctly viewed this attempt on the part of liberals to reconcile Christianity and modern scientific sensibilities as having emptied the Christian faith of anything really distinctive enough to require faith:

> [T]he liberal attempt at reconciling Christianity with modern science has really relinquished everything distinctive of Christianity, so that what remains is in essentials only that same indefinite type of religious aspiration which was in the world before Christianity came upon the scene. In trying to remove from Christianity everything that could possibly be objected to in the name of science . . . the apologist has really abandoned what he started out to defend.[2]

Beginning in 1910, religious conservatives published *The Fundamentals*. This publication, released as a series of twelve volumes for free distribution to Christian vocational and lay leaders, was an attempt to delineate and defend the fundamentals of Christian faith.[3] The series begins with several articles defending the traditional authorship and understanding of the Scriptures against the higher criticism[4] that had begun to take root in American seminaries and universities.

Following these articles concerning the trustworthiness and historical reliability of Scripture, several more take up the issue of Christ's unique status as God Incarnate, leading naturally into articles concerning the historicity of the Person of Christ, His virgin birth, and His true humanity. Then there are just a few works related to the Holy Spirit, emphasizing His personality and deity, followed by a long series of articles on salvation, beginning with the doctrine of sin and judgment, and continuing with articles on Christ's atonement, salvation by grace, regeneration, justification by faith, and the mandate toward evangelism and missions. The series concludes with several more articles discussing modern philosophies, religious cults, and several other ancillary topics.

Despite the rather obvious fact that these articles were a tract for their times, and therefore are situated to those times,[5] one may readily apprehend what was important to these early "fundamentalists." They prized their commitment to the absolute inspiration[6] and authority of Scripture, the full deity and true humanity of Christ, a Trinitarian understanding of God, the finality and sufficiency of Christ's death and (bodily) resurrection for our salvation, the need to appropriate that salvation by grace through faith alone, and the requirement to share that good news with those who stand in need of Christ. To these Defenders of the Faith, whom we shall refer to as the Classic Fundamentalists, what was considered worth defending was well understood.

Later Evangelicals

As the early fundamentalist coalition began to fracture, an increasing number of small church associations developed that held to a set of distinctive and shared convictions covering a fairly broad range of topics. Evangelicals who abandoned their mainline denominations also began effectively to abandon each other. It would appear that, having trained their polemical guns on the liberals for so long a period of time, and then having succeeded in putting structural distance between themselves and the liberals through the creation of separate denominations and educational institutions, they began to train their guns on each other.[7] Furthermore, evangelicals who had not yet aligned with fundamentalism as a separate movement were increasingly content to remain within their own apostate denominations when they began to witness the power struggles and multiplied divisions that afflicted the various fundamentalist organizations.[8] In their eyes, it seemed far more dignified, even strategic, to stay in and do battle with the liberal than to get out and quarrel with the militant. Perhaps even more worrisome was the prospect of actually taking on the more strident posture of the militant fundamentalist—of becoming just like him. All in all, deciding which was the supposed "Dark Side" was not always an easy thing to do in the poisoned atmosphere which blanketed the theological battlefields of the early to mid-twentieth century.

To counter these debilitating trends, increasingly more and more voices were heard calling the evangelical church to greater unity. Outside of fundamentalist churches, that effort has been largely successful as evangelicals have found or established avenues of cooperative ministry by means of parachurch groups, mission agencies, and publications. In fact, the effort has been so effective in bringing together great numbers of theologically diverse groups and individuals under the evangelical banner that a fairly recent "evangelical critique" has been taken up in order to awaken the evangelical camp to a growing theological tolerance which threatens to erode the entire enterprise at its very core. Like a large tree with diseased roots, evangelicalism is increasingly seen as an enterprise teeming with activity among its many branches, but threatened to be destroyed at its very base. If fundamentalism may be charged with an unwillingness to compromise on anything, the correction afforded by the broader evangelical movement may be seen as having compromised on too much. This development has led several prominent evangelical theologians and historians in recent years to revisit the question of what constitutes essential evangelicalism.

Mark Noll. Wheaton College professor Mark Noll may be credited as much as anyone with helping to sustain this evangelical critique near the close of the twentieth century, following earlier works by Francis Schaeffer and, to a lesser degree, Richard Quebedeaux, during the 1970s and 1980s. Toward the end of his book *The Scandal of the Evangelical Mind,* Noll invites the reader to travel the world and engage evangelicals in other cultures.[9] When we do that, we find that much of what is considered to be *essential* for evangelical faith in this country is really only the distinctive edge of a uniquely *American* evangelicalism—a movement, one might be quick to add, that has its roots in a fairly recent fundamentalist resurgence.

Perhaps some of those distinctly American views are due, at least in part, to a renewed emphasis on personal and post-graduate Bible study in this country, although to place much stock in that theory borders on hubris. It is difficult to deny the essence of what Noll is saying. Understanding what is essential to Christianity requires not only that one give attention to Scripture, but that one put distance between himself and more recent developments in Christian thought that have yet to be placed in their broader context, whether theologically, philosophically, geographically, or historically. We need to ask, for example, how our place in post-Enlightenment, Western civilization has helped to shape a more "scientific" approach to Scripture, and how that approach then shapes our cosmology and even eschatology.

Finally, when all is said and done, we need to ask how all of our systematic study in matters of cosmology and eschatology begins to remove our focus away from what is most important and essential to Christian faith. We need to ask how the buildup of settled convictions in so many theological areas begins to raise up barriers to other Christians who, in good conscience, may have dissented from our own closely held and "assured" views. With that as prelude, we turn now to those writers who recently have devoted considerable thought to the question of what is essential to evangelical faith.

George Marsden. Church historian George Marsden resolves what is perhaps essential to evangelical Christianity as follows: (1) belief in the "final authority" of the Bible; (2) belief in the "real, historical character of God's saving work recorded in Scripture"; (3) belief that salvation to eternal life is "based on the redemptive work of Christ"; (4) belief in the "importance of evangelism and missions"; and (5) belief in the "importance of a spiritually transformed life."[10] Marsden is willing even to distill from these essentials a more "economical" statement of essential evangelicalism: "that the sole authority in religion is the Bible and the sole means of salvation is a life-transforming experience wrought by the Holy Spirit through Faith in Jesus Christ."[11] Marsden's attempt at definition presumes certain key understandings, such as the true deity and real humanity of Christ. Orthodox tenets concerning the Person of Christ which evangelicals share with, say, Roman Catholicism and Eastern Orthodoxy, are thus tacitly assumed. That being true, his list is more a list of evangelical *distinctives* than *essentials*. To that degree, Marsden is less than helpful for our purposes.

D. A. Carson. Biblical scholar D. A. Carson is less apt to be misunderstood. In *The Gagging of God*, written while he was research professor of New Testament at Trinity Evangelical Divinity School, he begins by distinguishing "both a formal principle and a material principle" as defining evangelicalism. The formal principle is belief in the "truth, authority, and finality" of the Bible.[12] This emphasis corresponds to the opening set of articles in *The Fundamentals*. The material principle is belief in "the gospel [or, evangel] as understood in historic evangelical Protestantism." That means: (1) "Salvation is gained exclusively through personal faith in the finished cross-work of Jesus Christ, who is both God and man"; (2) "His atoning death . . . expiates our sin, vanquishes Satan, propitiates the Father, and inaugurates the promised kingdom"; (3) "In the ministry, death, resurrection, and exaltation of Jesus, God himself is supremely revealed, such that rejection of Jesus . . . [is] nothing less than rejection of God himself"; (4) "Christ has bequeathed the Holy Spirit, himself God, as the down payment of the final inheritance that will come to Christ's people when he himself returns"; (5) "The saving and transforming power of the Spirit displayed in the lives of Christ's people is the product of divine grace, grace alone — grace that is apprehended by faith alone"; and (6) "The knowledge of God that we enjoy becomes for us an impetus to missionary outreach characterized by urgency and compassion."[13]

Carson's summary of evangelical faith is further delineated through a series of qualifying statements regarding what evangelicalism is not. For our purpose, however, his affirmations of faith are more than sufficient, if not redundant. Among other things, one can distill something about the Trinity; Christ's Deity; His atoning death, resurrection, and exaltation; faith as the sole means by which one may appropriate what Christ has done to save us; the conversion experience as a work of the Holy Spirit; and a missionary mandate. Cast just a bit more generally, Carson develops the Person of Christ (items 1 and 3), His saving activity (items 1, 2, and 3), the manner in which that work is appropriated for salvation (items 1 and 5), the supernatural saving activity of the Holy Spirit in salvation (items 4 and 5), and the instrumental saving activity of man through proclamation (item 6).

Alister McGrath. British theologian Alister McGrath defines evangelicalism as "basically Christian orthodoxy, as set out in the ecumenical creeds, with a particular emphasis on the need for the personal assimilation and appropriation of faith and a marked reluctance to allow any matters of lesser importance to get in the way of the proclamation and application of the gospel."[14] Elsewhere, McGrath sets forth six fundamentals of evangelicalism as follows: (1) "The supreme authority of Scripture" as the Word of God; (2) "The majesty of Jesus Christ, both as incarnate God . . . and as the Savior of sinful humanity"; (3) "The lordship of the Holy Spirit"; (4) "The need for personal conversion"; (5) "The priority of evangelism"; and (6) "The importance of Christian community."[15] Under his second point, McGrath also deals with the centrality of the cross and the doctrine of justification "on account of Christ, through faith."[16] Moreover, the doctrine of the Trinity is at least implicit within McGrath's combined treatment of points (2) and (3), and of course it is explicit in the creeds to which he refers.

Randy Phillips. In a more popular venue, writing for the Promise Keepers in the forward to a book by E. Glenn Wagner, Randy Phillips lists five foundational convictions: (1) "The inerrancy of the Word of God"; (2) "The nature and attributes of God"; (3) "The Person and deity of Jesus Christ"; (4) "The role of the Holy Spirit in our salvation"; and (5) "Redemption and salvation through Jesus Christ."[17] Wagner himself is even less precise, writing in one place, "In my view all that is necessary to add to the Apostle's Creed and the Nicene Creed is the issue of the inerrancy of Scripture."[18] Both writers, while emphasizing orthodoxy *per se*, are less emphatic about what is distinctive within evangelicalism, perhaps reflecting the willingness of Promise Keepers to seek and promote unity among groups that are outside normative evangelicalism.

That completes our analysis of the several writers whose works comprised a recent "evangelical critique." Noll, Marsden, Carlson, McGrath, and Phillips are responding to a "felt need" for more definition within the movement to which they belong. The following table, while hardly precise, is helpful to summarize what these writers are willing to allow as comprising essential evangelicalism. For comparison, the early ecumenical Apostle's and Nicene creeds are also summarized as a combined entry, borrowing from our prior analysis in Chapter 2.

We learned at the beginning of this chapter that the early fundamentalists remained committed to the inspiration and authority of Scripture, the full deity and true humanity of Christ, a Trinitarian understanding of God, the finality and sufficiency of Christ's death and bodily resurrection for our salvation, the need to appropriate that salvation by grace through faith alone, and the requirement to share that good news with those who are lost. Evangelicals of the late twentieth century and on both sides of the Atlantic are in strong agreement, at least as they are represented by Carson and McGrath. This observation becomes especially true when Carson's "formal principle" regarding the authority of Scripture is included in the mix.

Table 1. Summary of Views Concerning Essential Evangelicalism.

Author	Nature of God	Person of Christ	Saving Work of Christ	Saving Role of Spirit	Req't of Faith	Need of Proclamation
Creeds[†]	✓	✓	✓			
Marsden[††]			✓	✓	✓	✓
Fundamentals	✓	✓	✓		✓	✓
Carson	✓	✓	✓	✓	✓	✓
McGrath	✓	✓	✓		✓	✓
Wagner	✓	✓	✓	✓		

[†] The Creeds also provide specificity regarding salvation-related themes (e.g., the Church, Second Coming, resurrection of the body, and immortality).

[††] Again, Marsden attempts to delineate what is *distinctive* vice *essential* about evangelicalism.

Ignoring that formal principle for the moment, and focusing instead upon the "material principle" of the Gospel, it can be seen that the fundamentalists and evangelicals of the last century remain in strong agreement with each other, as well with what we distilled as being the essence of early Protestant theology, represented in the historical creeds. Each stresses as essential a proper understanding of Jesus Christ,[19] His complete and sacrificial work for our salvation by death and resurrection, and our necessary response to that completed work—a faith apart from works. In describing the fundamentalist-evangelical phenomenon of the twentieth century, both Carson and McGrath note as well the importance of propagating the faith, but this more practical point is understandably missing from the formal theological treatises presented in the last two chapters.

The brief survey presented in this chapter has served us well, as far as it goes. Nevertheless, while we want to maintain a degree of sensitivity to what has been passed down through the historic creeds of the Church and the writings of our best and brightest theologians, still our final appeal must be made to the authoritative Scriptures. In the next chapter, then, we survey the apostolic witness to core Christianity as given to us in the New Testament.

Discussion Questions

1. What did the early liberals consider to be "essential" to Christian faith? Were they right? Why or why not?

2. In the view of the early fundamentalists, what beliefs needed to be emphasized and preserved in order to rescue Christianity from the liberals?

3. What was the basis for cooperation among the early fundamentalists? What is the basis for cooperation among self-professed fundamentalists today?

4. What did later evangelicals have in common with their fundamentalist forebears? How did they differ? Did those differences involve essential doctrines?

5. How might an understanding of recent fundamentalist and evangelical history help in setting down limits for cooperative ministry among Christians today?

Chapter 5

The New Testament Witness
To Core Christianity

Naturally, even had the various evangelical writers been absolutely homogeneous in their statements about essential evangelicalism, the final test of essential belief are the Scriptures themselves—deciding the content of essential Christianity is hardly a democratic process. What makes the following study all the more interesting are just these slight variances which we observe among committed evangelicals. Of course, it is altogether possible to make far too much of these differences. For the most part, Wagner and the early creeds affirm the same subset of beliefs for reasons already mentioned, and Marsden was not attempting to reiterate what is essential to shared Christian orthodoxy, only what is distinctive about evangelicalism.

Furthermore, because McGrath chooses not to include a statement regarding the role of the Holy Spirit in salvation has no bearing upon what he himself believes. Still, he chooses not to list these things when discussing essential belief. Neither should we overlook the overall agreement between Carson and McGrath. Both are as entrenched evangelicals as one can find anywhere, and both have a solid command of Scripture. Furthermore, both are essentially agreed that the early fundamentalists were correct in emphasizing what they did. That being true, there may exist a basic, biblical foundation to this shared understanding.

We are now prepared to make our appeal to Scripture. As was noted in the last chapter, while we do well to take an interest in what has been passed down through the historic creeds of the church and that literature produced by our fundamentalist and evangelical forbearers, still our final appeal must be the New Testament itself. Skipping past the four Gospels, we begin with the book of Acts as that book which contains the earliest examples of Christian practice immediately following the resurrection of Christ. We then continue with a careful look at the epistolary literature, as these are closest to being a normative guide for the practice of Christianity today.

In Acts

Throughout the book of Acts we are given insight into the essential content of apostolic teaching during the period of the church's infancy. Naturally, every occurrence of apostolic preaching that Luke records is set within its immediate context, and this historical milieu must be accounted before discovering what is substantial (*essential*) to the teaching at hand. Still, the text of Acts is well worth engaging, and often what is essential to a particular message can be had by comparing one message with another.

Peter on Pentecost. Peter's sermon before the Jews gathered in Jerusalem for Pentecost is recorded in Acts 2. God had just bestowed upon the apostles (and perhaps other believers) in Jerusalem a special ability to speak in foreign tongues, apparently to persuade these other Jews that what they taught was God-sanctioned and approved (cf. 1 Cor 14:22). Most reacted favorably; others, however, ridiculed the believers, accusing them of drunkenness (v. 13). In either case, Peter's next task was to corroborate what they had just observed by a straightforward proclamation of the truth—to explain the experience of these early followers of Jesus. What Peter will say, therefore, may fairly represent what is important to know and accept about the *Way*. It is core Christianity. If Luke's account of Peter's sermon is a condensed version of what Peter actually said, this point is all the more significant; presumably, what remains for the church in every age is that which Luke considers to be of primary importance:

> " 'In the last days, God says, I will pour out my Spirit
> on all people. Your sons and daughters will prophesy,
> your young men will see visions, your old men will

dream dreams. Even on my servants, both men and women, I will pour out my Spirit in those days, and they will prophesy. . . . And everyone who calls on the name of the Lord will be saved.' Men of Israel, listen to this: Jesus of Nazareth was a man accredited by God to you by miracles, wonders and signs, which God did among you through him, as you yourselves know. This man was handed over to you by God's set purpose and foreknowledge; and you, with the help of wicked men, put him to death by nailing him to the cross. But God raised him from the dead, freeing him from the agony of death, because it was impossible for death to keep its hold on him. David said about him: 'I saw the Lord always before me. Because he is at my right hand, I will not be shaken. Therefore my heart is glad and my tongue rejoices; my body also will live in hope, because you will not abandon me to the grave, nor will you let your Holy One see decay. You have made known to me the paths of life; you will fill me with joy in your presence.' Brothers, I can tell you confidently that the patriarch David died and was buried, and his tomb is here to this day. But he was a prophet and knew that God had promised him on oath that he would place one of his descendants on his throne. Seeing what was ahead, he spoke of the resurrection of the Christ, that he was not abandoned to the grave, nor did his body see decay. God has raised this Jesus to life, and we are all witnesses of the fact. Exalted to the right hand of God, he has received from the Father the promised Holy Spirit and has poured out what you now see and hear. For David did not ascend to heaven, and yet he said, 'The Lord said to my Lord: "Sit at my right hand until I make your enemies a footstool for your feet." ' Therefore let all Israel be assured of this: God has made this Jesus, whom you crucified, both Lord and Christ." When the people heard this, they were cut to the heart and said to Peter and the other apostles, "Brothers, what shall we do?" Peter replied, "Repent and be baptized, every one of you, in the name of Jesus Christ for the forgiveness of your sins. And you will receive the gift of the Holy Spirit" (Acts 2:17-38).

Given his predominantly Jewish audience, Peter introduces his subject by noting how the prophet Joel had predicted that God would pour out His Spirit upon His people, that they would prophesy (vv. 17-21), and that before the end of the age, everyone would have opportunity to be saved by calling on the name of the Lord. That having been established, Peter moves directly into the substance of His sermon: that Jesus was accredited as to His Person by miracles, wonders, and signs (v. 22); that He died on the cross and was raised from the dead (vv. 23-32); and that He was exalted to the right hand of God, whereupon He has "poured out what you now see and hear" (v. 33). All that Peter has proclaimed thus far is the explanation for the experience of tongues. But Peter is not finished. Because of these things, he says, "God has made this Jesus . . . both Lord and Christ" (v. 36), such that there is forgiveness of sins through repentance and baptism in the name of Jesus (v. 38).

When separated from the context of tongues-speaking in which it is found, Peter's proclamation of core, apostolic Christianity may be summarized as follows: Jesus is the crucified, risen, and ascended Lord and Christ, and salvation can be had in His name. In other words, Peter speaks to the Person and salvific work of Christ, and to how individuals can appropriate that salvation through a personal response of repentance and baptism.[1] Perhaps incidental to this proclamation, but no less apparent, is his evident trinitarianism as demonstrated by a concurrent mention of God, the Holy Spirit, and the Lord Jesus.

Peter at the temple gate. Peter's sermon at the temple gate is recorded in Acts 3. Peter had just healed a man who had been crippled from birth. When Jewish onlookers reacted with amazement at what had happened, Peter began to preach:

When Peter saw this, he said to them: "Men of Israel, why does this surprise you? Why do you stare at us as if by our own power or godliness we had made this man walk? The God of Abraham, Isaac and Jacob, the God of our fathers, has glorified his servant Jesus. You handed him over to be killed, and you disowned him before Pilate, though he had decided to let him go. You disowned the Holy and Righteous One and asked that a murderer be released to you. You killed the author of life, but God raised him from the dead. We are witnesses of this. By faith in the name of Jesus, this man whom you see and know was made strong. It is Jesus' name and the faith that comes through him that has given this complete healing to him, as you can all see. Now, brothers, I know that you acted in ignorance, as did your leaders. But this is how God fulfilled what he had foretold through all the prophets, saying that his Christ would suffer. Repent, then, and turn to God, so that your sins may be wiped out, that times of refreshing may come from the Lord, and that he may send the Christ, who has been appointed for you—even Jesus" (Acts 3:12-20).

Again, Peter's task was to explain their experience of what had just happened. As before, his audience is Jewish so that he begins with "the God of Abraham, Isaac, and Jacob, the God of our fathers" (v. 13). In connection with Israel's God, Peter preaches Jesus as the servant of God (v. 13), the Holy and Righteous One (v. 14), and the author of life (v. 15). He uniquely identifies Jesus as the one who has died and was raised from the dead (v. 15). Furthermore, he testifies that it was the crippled man's faith in Jesus' name that had caused him to be healed (v. 16). But turning to the greater spiritual need amongst the crowd, Peter advises his audience regarding their necessary response to his message—"Repent, then, and turn to God, so that your sins may be wiped out" (v. 19). Here, in light of his Jewish audience and the Hebrew Scriptures, Peter adds something concerning the future return of Christ from heaven (presupposing His ascension) and the restoration of all things under Him.

Peter's message is conditioned once again by the circumstances in which he finds himself; nevertheless, when detached from the exigencies of speaking to a Jewish audience, for whom special emphasis is made regarding the prophets and the special covenant relationship that exists between God and Israel, Peter's proclamation of core, apostolic Christianity may be summarized as follows: Jesus is the crucified, risen, and ascended Holy and Righteous One, and the author of life through whom salvation can be had by repenting and turning to God by faith. In other words, Peter again speaks to the Person and salvific work of Christ, and how individuals can appropriate that salvation through a personal response of faith. Peter's reference to the covenant God of Israel ensures continuity with the entirety of the Old Testament's witness to Him, and Christ's "connectedness" to this God speaks to His own divine nature as the "Holy and Righteous One" and "author of life."

Peter before the Sanhedrin. The bulk of Peter's sermon before the Jewish Sanhedrin is recorded in Acts 4, although a substantial addendum is provided in Acts 5. After Peter and John had been arrested and imprisoned overnight for having healed the crippled man, they were brought before the religious leaders for questioning:

> Then Peter, filled with the Holy Spirit, said to them: "Rulers and elders of the people! If we are being called to account today for an act of kindness shown to a cripple and are asked how he was healed, then know this, you and all the people of Israel: It is by the name of Jesus Christ of Nazareth, whom you crucified but whom God raised from the dead, that this man stands before you healed. He is 'the stone you builders rejected, which has become the capstone.' Salvation is found in no one else, for there is no other name under heaven given to men by which we must be saved" (Acts 4:8-12).

70

In response to an inquiry into the source of their miraculous power to heal the crippled man, Peter testified that it was by the name of Jesus Christ. He identified Jesus as the one crucified but whom God raised from the dead (v. 10), and as the one for whom it could be said, "Salvation is found in no one else, for there is no other name under heaven given to men by which we must be saved" (v. 12). Later, Peter and the other apostles again proclaimed before the Sanhedrin that Jesus had died but that God had raised Him from the dead and "exalted him to his own right hand as Prince and Savior that he might give repentance and forgiveness of sins to Israel" (Acts 5:30-31).

Peter's proclamation of core Christianity may be summarized as follows: Jesus is the crucified, risen, and ascended (exalted) Prince[2] and Savior, such that salvation can only be had in His name. As for how that salvation is appropriated, repentance and forgiveness of sins are a gift of God. So Peter speaks to the Person and salvific work of Christ, and to how individuals can appropriate that salvation through a personal response of repentance as they are enabled by God. As seems apparent in every case, Peter evidences a trinitarian understanding of God as demonstrated by his concurrent mention of God, the Holy Spirit, and Jesus as Prince and Savior (esp. Acts 5:31-32).

Peter with Cornelius. Further into Acts, we find Peter before Cornelius, a God-fearing Gentile who yet needed to be saved as confirmed by his own subsequent testimony (Acts 11:14):

> Then Peter began to speak: "I now realize how true it is that God does not show favoritism but accepts men from every nation who fear him and do what is right. You know the message God sent to the people of Israel, telling the good news of peace through Jesus Christ, who is Lord of all. You know what has happened throughout Judea, beginning in Galilee after the baptism that John preached—how God anointed Jesus of Nazareth with the Holy Spirit and power, and how he went around doing good and healing all

who were under the power of the devil, because God
was with him. We are witnesses of everything he did
in the country of the Jews and in Jerusalem. They
killed him by hanging him on a tree, but God raised
him from the dead on the third day and caused him
to be seen. He was not seen by all the people, but
by witnesses whom God had already chosen—by
us who ate and drank with him after he rose from
the dead. He commanded us to preach to the people
and to testify that he is the one whom God appointed
as judge of the living and the dead. All the prophets
testify about him that everyone who believes in him
receives forgiveness of sins through his name" (Acts
10:34-43).

Peter proclaims to him "the good news of peace through Jesus
Christ, who is Lord of all" (Acts 10:36). He goes on to explain that
God had anointed Jesus with the Holy Spirit and power (v. 38) such
that He went about doing good and healing people, that He had been
crucified and yet raised on the third day, and that He was made to be
judge of the living and the dead (vv. 39-41). Again for Peter, the call
for a response was a vital component of his preaching: "Everyone
who believes in him receives forgiveness of sins through his name"
(v. 43).

By now, the fundamental pattern of Peter's preaching is well
attested—he speaks to the Person of Christ (He is Lord of all), the
salvific work of Christ (He lived a righteous life, died, and was raised
from the dead), and to how individuals can appropriate that salvation (i.e., receive forgiveness of sins) through a personal response of
faith in Christ. As before, Peter's trinitarianism is understood by His
reference to Jesus as Lord of all, anointed by the Holy Spirit, and
appointed by God (i.e., the Father).

Paul at Pisidian Antioch. In Acts 13, it is Paul that stands up to
preach in the Jewish synagogue. He begins with a short history of
God's dealings with the Jews, culminating in God's exaltation of
David as king:

"From this man's descendants God has brought to Israel the Savior Jesus, as he promised. Before the coming of Jesus, John preached repentance and baptism to all the people of Israel. As John was completing his work, he said: 'Who do you think I am? I am not that one. No, but he is coming after me, whose sandals I am not worthy to untie.' Brothers, children of Abraham, and you God-fearing Gentiles, it is to us that this message of salvation has been sent. The people of Jerusalem and their rulers did not recognize Jesus, yet in condemning him they fulfilled the words of the prophets that are read every Sabbath. Though they found no proper ground for a death sentence, they asked Pilate to have him executed. When they had carried out all that was written about him, they took him down from the tree and laid him in a tomb. But God raised him from the dead, and for many days he was seen by those who had traveled with him from Galilee to Jerusalem. They are now his witnesses to our people. We tell you the good news: What God promised our fathers he has fulfilled for us, their children, by raising up Jesus. As it is written in the second Psalm: 'You are my Son; today I have become your Father.' The fact that God raised him from the dead, never to decay, is stated in these words: 'I will give you the holy and sure blessings promised to David.' So it is stated elsewhere: 'You will not let your Holy One see decay.' For when David had served God's purpose in his own generation, he fell asleep; he was buried with his fathers and his body decayed. But the one whom God raised from the dead did not see decay. Therefore, my brothers, I want you to know that through Jesus the forgiveness of sins is proclaimed to you. Through him everyone who believes is justified from everything you could not be justified from by the law of Moses" (Acts 13:23-39).

Paul's basic message portrays Jesus as the Savior of Israel, born in the line of David (v. 23), and as one who had been executed without just cause, but was raised from the dead by God such that now "through Jesus the forgiveness of sins is proclaimed to you" (v. 38). Paul, no less than Peter, makes very clear how it is that one may be forgiven of his sins: "Through [Jesus] everyone who believes is justified from everything you could not be justified from by the law of Moses" (v. 39). Here, as in every place in Acts, the essential Christian proclamation is the same—*this* is who Jesus really is, *this* is what He did to save us, and *this* is what you must do to be saved. Whenever there is a direct disclosure of the apostolic proclamation in Acts, this is the established pattern.

Table 2, below, summarizes what has been demonstrated in Acts to be essential to the Christian faith. The essential message of the apostolic witness in the book of Acts concerned the Person of Christ, what he did to save us in his death, resurrection and ascension, and how we must respond to that finished work in order to be saved. While not explicitly proclaimed, it is everywhere at least minimally assumed that God is an economic Trinity.[3] Finally, we can at least surmise from the apostles' own *pattern* of preaching that an essential characteristic of Christian faith is the necessity of proclaiming that apostolic message. When compared with the views concerning essential evangelicalism identified in Table 1, McGrath, Carson, and *The Fundamentals* are closest to the record in Acts.

> The essential Christian proclamation is the same—*this* is who Jesus really is, *this* is what He did to save us, and *this* is what you must do to be saved.

Conspicuous by its absence in Acts is the importance of understanding the role of the Holy Spirit in salvation. While Acts 5:31 may clearly identify the response of saving faith ("repentance") as being a gift of God, the Holy Spirit *per se* is not mentioned, except that He is given to those who obey Him (v. 32). Likewise in Acts 2, the Holy Spirit is received by those already identified as having responded to the proclamation of salvation in

Christ (v. 38). Apparently, while a proper understanding of the Holy Spirit's role in salvation is a matter of earnest inquiry, it is not part of the *kerygma*, the essential message of the apostles.

Table 2. Summary of the Apostolic Message in Acts.

Passage	Nature of God	Person of Christ	Saving Work of Christ	Saving Role of Spirit	Req't of Faith	Need of Procla-mation
Acts 2	(✓)	✓	✓		✓†	(✓)
Acts 3	(✓)	✓	✓		✓	(✓)
Acts 4, 5	(✓)	✓	✓		✓	(✓)
Acts 10	(✓)	✓	✓		✓	(✓)
Acts 13	(✓)	✓	✓		✓	(✓)

† As mentioned previously, Peter preaches forgiveness of sins through repentance *and baptism* in the name of Jesus Christ. What is important for our purpose is that his proclamation includes the manner in which Christ's salvific work may be individually appropriated.

Perhaps here is a good place to remind ourselves of that which we have set out to do. In surveying the book of Acts, we have determined to know what was *essential* to the apostolic understanding of Christian faith, assuming that what is essential may be known by what is proclaimed. Our emphasis upon what the apostles preached is not to deny that other areas of doctrine (e.g., the role of the Holy Spirit in salvation) have a legitimate place in the broader Christian understanding of things, nor that these other doctrines cannot be held with conviction and maintained as part of what is *distinctive* to a particular Christian body. Nor is that emphasis an attempt to deny what is patently true of Christian churches and church groups generally, that closer bonds can and do (and should) arise among Christians for whom broad agreement exists on a relatively wide base of subjects.

The question remains, however, as to whether anyone may object on biblical grounds to some form of limited ecumenism among evangelicals for whom real differences do exist on non-essential issues, even while non-negotiable essentials are held in common. In other words, are "hard-line" separatists legitimate in their insistence upon doctrinal homogeneity among Christian groups seeking to engage in cooperative ministry? Can a church cooperate with another church outside its own immediate fellowship or association, say, on essential evangelism, even while maintaining to itself what is doctrinally *distinctive*? With these questions as our motivating guide, the need to continue a survey of the New Testament literature becomes all the more apparent.

In the Pauline Corpus

The book of Acts, like the Gospels, is primarily narrative. What we observe in the narrative literature is more *descriptive* of apostolic proclamation than *prescriptive*. Still, the shear repetition of similar elements in the recorded sermons of Peter and Paul required an examination of the material in Acts. Having said that, it is the didactic (instructional) literature contained in the Epistles that helps to formulate or set out in more concrete fashion what is narrated in Acts. Risking a bit of reductionism, we may say that the Epistles prescribe what the Gospels and Acts describe.

First Corinthians and Galatians. What is remarkable about the opening chapter of 1 Corinthians is what it reveals about the differences that existed among the believers in the Corinthian assembly, as shown by the many factions that existed within the church. Paul clearly did not approve of these factions; in fact, he rebuked the Corinthians for their many divisions. Still, he does not address who is right or wrong, or why such divisions even exist. Paul is not interested in deciding and adjudicating their differences, to mark out who among them are the erring brethren. Details concerning their differences are not even recorded, presumably because Paul himself is not so much concerned with what those differences are. Instead, he commands them simply to agree with one another (v. 10). He exhorts them to bury their differences and come together.

The reason Paul is so unconcerned about such apparently real disparities is subsequently made clear—despite the differences that

76

keep them apart, enough substantial agreement already exists to draw them together. It is what matters to Paul, it is what matters to the Gospel, and it is what is essential and basic to everything else that goes on at Corinth and in every assembly: "Jesus Christ and Him crucified" (1 Cor 2:2). Paul wrote that the "Jews demand miraculous signs and Greeks look for wisdom, but *we preach Christ crucified*" (1 Cor 1:22-23a). Everything else flows from that central truth. For Christians living in a hostile world, very little else matters.

In the churches of Galatia, however, something was critically wrong. When Paul writes to the churches of Galatia, he immediately points up an issue of doctrine. Here Paul gives no ground whatsoever. He does not ask that all the believers bury their differences and learn to get along; instead, he asks that every believer get in line with apostolic teaching. The reason becomes abundantly clear. Paul writes with regard to the Judaizing tendency that had begun to infect the Galatian churches. Some teachers had begun to corrupt the Gospel by adding to faith the requirements of the Law. At issue, in other words, was the precise manner in which the unsaved may appropriate what God had done in Christ to save them, and thus to *be* saved. That corruption of salvific truth was to Paul "another gospel." Paul recognized that what was at stake in this instance was *essential* Christianity. It was one thing to *obscure* the Gospel, quite another to *obviate* the Gospel.

One passage in 1 Corinthians requires special attention for the way that it appears to encapsulate or summarize the core commitments of Christian faith:

> Now, brothers, I want to remind you of the gospel I preached to you, which you received and on which you have taken your stand. By this gospel you are saved, if you hold firmly to the word I preached to you. Otherwise, you have believed in vain. For what I received I passed on to you *as of first importance*:[4] that Christ died for our sins according to the Scriptures, that he was buried, that he was raised on the third day according to the Scriptures (1 Cor 15:1-4).

Paul continues with a list of various historical witnesses to the resurrection of Christ, but the substantive content of what he writes as inclusive of the "gospel" is already complete—the death, burial, and resurrection of Christ. Moreover, it is this Gospel that is most important when stacked up again any other of Paul's teachings. The Gospel has absolute priority over every other teaching just because it is at the center of and therefore most essential to Christian belief.

Furthermore, Paul leaves us little doubt that what he had just written constituted the very essence of his apostolic ministry among the Corinthians: ". . . This is what we preach, and this is what you believed" (1 Cor 15:11). The Corinthian church was established around a single organizing principle: belief in the crucified, buried, and risen Lord Jesus Christ. Any other teaching, however true, was secondary to the fundamental truths concerning Christ. That is not to deny the importance of biblical instruction in "the whole will of God" (Acts 20:27), nor of the need to seek after maturity beyond "the elementary teachings about Christ" (Heb 6:1-2). Those are the issues that we will take up in Chapter 10. But these other doctrines and practices are simply not to be the pretext for the kind of disunity and dismemberment which the Body of Christ increasingly must endure.

> While all truth is traceable back to God Himself, some truths are nevertheless more important than others. These are the truths which serve to discriminate what is Christian from what is not.

So while all truth is traceable back to God Himself, some truths are nevertheless more important than others. These are the truths which serve to discriminate what is Christian from what is not. There is such a thing as primary or essential truth, and it is that truth which deals specifically with Christ and salvation (v. 2), acceptance of which makes one Christian. It stands to reason that other non-salvific truths are secondary or non-essential, simply because they address secondary matters. So while separating truths into essentials and non-essentials may not be popular within certain strains of fundamentalism, it characterized the ministry of Paul.

First Timothy. The book of 1 Timothy is a Pastoral Epistle of Paul, written to Timothy, Paul's "true son in the faith." Once a traveling missionary companion of Paul, but now the pastor of the church at Ephesus, Timothy needed instruction regarding his leadership role in the church. Paul wastes little space before reminding Timothy what was essential to their shared message and ministry: "Here is a trustworthy saying that deserves full acceptance: Christ Jesus came into the world to save sinners" (1 Tim 1:15). In light of that central pronouncement, Paul then exhorts Timothy to pray for everyone, and especially for rulers and those in authority. The reason, Paul says, is because "this . . . pleases God our Savior, who wants all men to be saved and to come to a knowledge of the truth" (1 Tim 2:3-4). Already, then, the central and essential message of apostolic Christianity was that God is a Savior who wants everyone to be saved, and He had already made that salvation possible by sending Jesus Christ into the world to save sinners.

Had Paul stopped right there, we would already have understood fairly well what he considered to be the non-negotiable, essential truths of Christianity. But Paul continues to explicate what he means by what he says: "For there is one God and one mediator between God and men, the man Christ Jesus, who gave himself as a ransom for all men—the testimony given in its proper time. And *for this purpose* I was appointed a herald and an apostle" (1 Tim 2:5-7a). Paul had been appointed an apostle that he might testify to the saving grace of God in Christ Jesus.

That is not to suggest that Paul cared little to exhort and remind Timothy of the many other aspects of the ministry to which he must take heed. Paul did. However, this does suggest very strongly what Paul considered to be the *essence* of apostolic Christianity. In fact, in the direct context of warnings to Timothy about false teachers, Paul identifies what he understands as comprising "sound doctrine." Namely, it is that teaching which "conforms to the glorious gospel of the blessed God" (1 Tim 1:11). For Paul, a "truth-teller" was simply one whose message corresponded to that apostolic proclamation which centered upon Jesus Christ.[5]

Before leaving the book of 1 Timothy, one additional passage requires comment. A standard proof-text for biblical inspiration and authority is part of Paul's exhortation to young Timothy: "But as for you, continue in what you have learned and have become convinced of, because you know those from whom you learned it, and how from infancy you have known the holy Scriptures, *which are able to make you wise for salvation through faith in Christ Jesus.* All Scripture is God-breathed and is useful for teaching, rebuking, correcting and training in righteousness, so that the man of God may be thoroughly equipped for every good work" (2 Tim 3:14-17). When dealing with this passage, the usual emphasis is placed upon vv. 16-17; there, the doctrine of inspiration is set forth and explained as to its practical utility. One purpose of Scripture, in fact, is that "the man of God may be thoroughly equipped for every good work." The more overarching and primary purpose clause, however, is given in the preceding verse: Scripture is that which can "make you wise for salvation through faith in Christ Jesus." Once again, the emphasis in 1 Timothy is upon the saving (and sanctifying) purpose of the Bible.

Other passages

While other passages address the question at hand, two additional passages especially bear mentioning, one outside the Pauline corpus. John writes concerning how we ought to ascertain whether a messenger is truly from God, since many false prophets had begun to appear and lead people astray: "This is how you can recognize the Spirit of God: Every spirit that acknowledges that Jesus Christ has come in the flesh is from God" (1 John 4:2). While delimited by its literary and historical context, what Paul dealt with concerned the nature of Christ's Person. In this instance, perhaps Paul had already to deal with incipient tendencies toward Cerinthian and Docetist forms of Gnosticism.[6] Paul dealt with a similar problem among the Corinthians: "Therefore I tell you that no one who is speaking by the Spirit of God says, 'Jesus be cursed,' and no one can say, 'Jesus is Lord,' except by the Holy Spirit" (1 Cor 12:3). There he dealt with certain direct implications of the Holy Spirit's work in salvation. Both John and Paul are willing to demand uniformity of belief when failure to do so would malign their understanding of Christ and salvation.

From a survey of several New Testament passages outside of the Gospels and Acts, then, what we ascertained to be true of "essential" or core Christianity from the book of Acts remains intact, if not dramatically confirmed. The apostles required unity around a shared understanding of who Christ is, what He did to save us, and what we must do to be saved. At Panama Baptist Church, where I serve as Senior Pastor, we have distilled these three facets of core Christianity even further: Christ,[7] Cross, and Conversion. To be sure, the apostles taught on many other theological and practical interests, including the ecclesiastical, eschatological, and pneumatological.[8] However, never do they identify these issues as providing or contributing to the essential basis for cooperative fellowship and ministry among believers.

In the next section, we look at how our understanding of core Christianity may condition the way we interact with other Christians outside our own faith tradition, as well as how that understanding may change the way that we carry out our own mission within the context of our own local church. Among other issues, we will also look at the continuing need to teach distinctive doctrine, along with the practicality of doing so. Having grabbed onto the importance of knowing what is essential to Christian faith in no way implies a need to grow some kind of a "least common denominator" ministry.

Discussion Questions

1. What role should Scripture play in determining what is essential to Christian faith?

2. It has been assumed in this book that what the apostles *proclaimed* must be that which is *essential* to Christian faith. Is this a valid assumption? Why or why not?

3. If certain teachings, while perhaps biblical, are not essential to faith, what role should they play in the life of your church? How should they affect your dealings with other churches?

4. From your reading thus far, state in your own words what teachings are essential to Christian faith. Does your church profess and teach these things?

5. Based upon your present understanding of what is essential to Christian faith, are you a Christian? If not, what must happen in order for you to become a Christian right now?

Part Two

Living Out the Core

Chapter 6

Application to Inter-Church Ministry, Part 1

—ɯ—

At this point, we are prepared to apply what we have learned about essential Christianity to the very practical question of how to engage in Christian ministry, both within the independent church and among churches. If the case from Scripture is as clear as was suggested here, why do so many fundamentalists insist upon closing themselves off from a wider fellowship of evangelicals? Why do some Christians choose instead to wall themselves in and remain aloof from so many others who share their belief in Christ—who affirm His essential deity, His sacrificial death for sins, His bodily resurrection and ascension, and the specific requirement of repentance and faith in Christ alone for the forgiveness of sins? How is it that some Christians, while admitting that we will all be in heaven together someday, cannot cooperate or fellowship together in the here and now? These are questions that must be answered fairly, and with due consideration to the sensitivities of our fundamentalist brethren.

Part of the answer to that question may lie within the characteristic human weaknesses that plague us all—pride of ownership, personality conflicts, and the like. To be fair, however, the other part of the answer may lie in Scripture. Many fundamentalists appeal to distinct (and well-memorized) passages in Scripture as obligating them to maintain their existing wall of separation from "erring" brethren. The perimeter fences around Pastor James' church in the first chapter may have been imaginary, but they were no less real. It is Scripture more than anything else that serves as a pretext and parameter for fellowship and cooperation. This chapter and the next, among other things, provides an examination of several New

Testament passages to determine whether they teach the brand of separatism being practiced today.

One of the more contentious issues among fundamentalists is the degree to which a church may cooperate or fellowship with another church that holds a different view in one or more areas of doctrine. Some churches remain completely aloof from other churches, almost proud in their independence and autonomy. Other churches belong to regional or national associations of churches, in which there is at least as much doctrinal homogeneity as already exists at the local level.[1] The real question is what can be done in numerous small, isolated towns, for example, where such kindred associations are impractical or non-existent. Can a cessationist (with reference to tongues-speaking), independent Bible Church or Baptist Church or Community Church find any ground for mutual fellowship or ministry with, say, the local Assemblies of God? To answer that question, we must first determine the biblical grounds for separating churches from each other. Hint: it has something to do with core Christianity!

The separation standard

As stated earlier, many self-styled fundamentalists gladly affirm that church groups outside their own may claim and use the Christian name, nevertheless their strong distaste for "compromise" leads them to a strict practice of ecclesiastical separatism even from among those who agree with them upon the Christian essentials. Despite what we have learned about the core commitments of apostolic Christianity, that which is essential to Christian confession, these would insist that agreement must be had in virtually every area of doctrine before any formal, visible unity were to take place.

A critique of this rather extreme stance virtually necessitates a short review of the book by Ernest Pickering that upholds that position. In *Biblical Separation—the Struggle for a Pure Church*, Pickering dealt specifically with separation on an ecclesiastical level. His book remains a standard text for many in independent circles who would claim to be consistent (secondary) separatists.[2] While not every reader will be familiar with this work, a brief interaction with it will prove beneficial as an introduction to what has become the canon of behavior among so many separatist-minded Christians.

In his book, Pickering attempts a full-scale apologetic for the brand of separatism that has characterized much of North American fundamentalism during the twentieth century. His approach is generally commendable, avoiding as he does the usually superficial proof-texting that attends a typical apologetic for biblical separation. In fact, Pickering marshals considerable support to conclude that biblical unity and love in Christ can be expressed apart from substantive theological compromise, and without the false unity afforded by denominational structures. Also to his credit, Pickering is careful to stress that the difference between separatism and inclusivism is one of priority rather than opposing views of truth. In fact, Pickering is correct in his observation that, while a separatist tendency may have been somewhat *distinctive* of early fundamentalists, it was not an *essential* characteristic of that movement.

The greatest issue surrounding the doctrine of separation, then, is deciding upon what ground it becomes necessary. With regard to this primary question, Pickering warns that "great care must be taken in implementing the doctrine of separation lest one be ship-wrecked on the shoals of human pettiness."[3] Moving to the opposite extreme, Pickering documents how leading evangelicals have so liberally drawn the lines as to render biblical separation untenable. He quotes Ockenga as counseling for denominational unity "unless that denomination has *officially* repudiated Biblical Christianity" (p. 121, emphasis mine). Likewise, he cites Carnell's definition of apostasy: "If a denomination removes the gospel from its creed or confession, or if it leaves the gospel but removes the believer's right to preach it, the believer may justly conclude that the denomination is apostate" (p. 136). Surely Pickering is correct in his view that "apostasy must be defined in terms of what apostates believe and do, not in terms of what they allow others to do" (p. 162). In this way, the book offers some valid criticisms against early leaders of the modern-day evangelical resurgence.

But whereas Pickering succeeds in at least bounding the problem, he is far less clear in communicating the precise point of departure for the biblical separatist. It is this uncertainty among fundamentalists in general which probably leads many to "err on the side of caution." In one place, Pickering implies very strongly that fellowship must be predicated upon a shared view of creationism and biblical inspiration. But is this creationism in general, or *young earth* creationism, that which most modern-day (post-Morris)[4] fundamentalists seem to insist upon as a test of fellowship? Would Dr. Pickering have allowed into his fellowship the likes of James Orr or Cyrus Scofield, both of whom were pioneering and tireless fundamentalists, and both of whom were at least open to old earth creationism? More on this issue a bit later.

As to the latter concern, one can only assume that by raising the doctrine of inspiration, Pickering is referring to the ongoing crisis on *inerrancy*. The point being made is that defining the boundaries for fellowship is essential to any practical argument for separation. Without definition, the whole enterprise becomes just a little academic, and as soon as one moves beyond the essentials, it would appear that nothing may be withheld as grounds for separating from equally committed brethren.

In fact, Pickering appears ready and willing to insist upon complete doctrinal homogeneity. For example, he suggests that "the unity of the faith . . . is an *entire system* of divinely revealed truth" (p. 184, emphasis mine). And again, Pickering writes about those having "incomplete knowledge . . . of *some teaching of Scripture*," stating that we "should not merely continue to fellowship with them as those who have done nothing wrong" (p. 221). Doubtless these statement have some merit, but they require further definition, and a whole lot of nuancing, both of which Pickering fails to provide. Will dissent on a single issue disqualify one from fellowship within the fold? Are there not certain Christian *essentials* upon which proper fellowship can be based? By the author's own admission, it is a *schismatic* that "sees every doctrine as equally important" (p. 208).

That is not to suggest that Pickering doesn't at least ask the right question. He does. Indeed, he asks, "What are the doctrinal limitations beyond which one cannot go in fellowship?" (p. 222). The problem is that he does not subsequently define those doctrinal limits. Pickering argues for separation "when vital doctrines of the

Christian faith are rejected and heterodox views are either embraced or tolerated" (p. 186), yet we are not told what those vital doctrines might include. He writes of "vital convictions" (p. 226), and yet we are not told what those convictions might be. In fact, his whole appeal to "vital" issues appears overturned when he subsequently counsels for "considerable agreement" between churches regarding doctrine (p. 227). In summary, Pickering cautions against being too extreme in the practice of ecclesiastical separation, but never provides substance to fill those cautions with practical significance. This ambivalence is precisely where our foregoing scriptural analysis may serve to properly define the *biblical* limits of fellowship, and save us all from unnecessary division.

The separatist legacy

The need for such definition cannot be overstated. Over the past couple of decades, Pickering's own fellowship of Regular Baptist churches has lost more churches to zealously separatist pastors and congregations than it has been able to gain in new churches, as Figure 2 demonstrates. Because of such ambivalence toward readily apparent abuses within separatist movements, vocal KJV-only factions[5] continue to set brother against brother, strident five-point Calvinists continue to break from their Calvinistic brethren, and at least a few popularizers of young-earth creationism continue to lambaste the views of old-earth creationists as hopelessly bound up with the prevailing assumptions of atheistic and naturalistic evolution. As a result, Regular Baptist churches may well continue to decline in number. Clearly, there is a better, more biblical approach to deciding one's basis for fellowship. At Panama Baptist Church, we have a stake in that decision, as we gladly choose to affiliate with the GARBC.

Figure 2. Churches in the GARBC.[6]

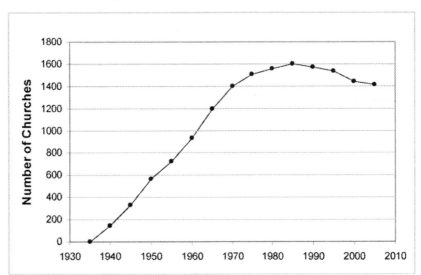

As alluded to earlier, one issue that divides Christians today, and which serves as a suitable case study for an examination of current separatist practice, is the question of origins. Indeed, this issue may be paradigmatic of several other theological divisions that plague the fundamentalist churches. In recent times, belief in a recent, literal six-day creation has become another litmus test for fellowship. By this test, most fundamental churches today would not be able to cooperate with the venerable Saint Augustine, though he is quoted repeatedly and favorably in many of those same churches (in more Calvinistic and Reformed circles). Some 1,500 years ago, Augustine felt it necessary to regard the six days of creation as representing something other than an ordinary day: "We must bear in mind that these [ordinary] days indeed recall the days of creation, but without in any way being really similar to them."[7]

By the same reasoning, in fact, these same fundamental churches would not have been able to cooperate even with some of those theological forebears who may be credited with giving them the "Fundamentalist" label to start with. Early Classic Fundamentalists were open to less traditional interpretations of Genesis—a point of fact that most fundamentalists today would feel just a little scandalized to learn. This fact is all the more surprising, given that these early fundamentalists were evangelical orthodoxy's belligerent, forward defense against a rising tide of theological liberalism.

Two prominent defenders of Christian orthodoxy come immediately to mind. George Frederick Wright, writing in *The Fundamentals* (c. 1910), says that "the world was not made in an instant, or even in a day (*whatever period day may signify*) but in six days. Throughout the whole *process* there was an orderly progress from lower to higher forms of matter and life" [emphases mine]. Respected theologian B. B. Warfield of Princeton Theological Seminary, author of *The Inspiration and Authority of the Bible*, defender of biblical inerrancy, and himself a contributor to *The Fundamentals*, is at least as clear in allowing for evolutionary development as the means by which God created the diversity of living things.[8] Bear in mind, these are not representatives of the so-called New Evangelicalism in the mid- to late-twentieth century[9] that have been charged repeatedly with retreat and compromise by the fundamentalist press. Instead, they are turn-of-the-century, articulate defenders of orthodox and evangelical Christianity at the very outset of the modernist-fundamentalist controversy.

Well before the publication of Ernest Pickering's *Biblical Separation*, Pickering's own beloved GARBC had gone on record rejecting the impulse by some, at least, to require that every pastor or church in fellowship with the association be required to espouse young-earth creationism. A resolution concerning creation passed on June 21, 1966, at the GARBC National Conference in Grand Rapids, Michigan. Conspicuous by its absence was any stipulated belief in a literal 24-hour creative day, though it had been debated before final passage of the motion. With reference to the 24-hour view, the resolution explicitly stated that "we would not . . . wish to exclude from Associational fellowship those holding other views." Most present-day Regular Baptists appear totally unaware of that milestone decision in the life of their Fellowship.[10]

Even the venerated *Scofield Reference Bible* leaves room for a vaguely defined creative day as being "a period of time marked off by a beginning and ending."[11] Neither Wright, B. B. Warfield, nor those with whom they collaborated to defend apostolic Christianity and for whom the term *fundamentalist* was coined, considered one's view on the modus operandi of creation to be a litmus test of fidelity to the Christian Scriptures, much less a test of fellowship among like-minded evangelicals. By contrast, most fundamentalists today consider any defection away from consistent belief in young-earth creationism to be a breach of orthodoxy, punishable by censure or dismissal. The evangelical has not drifted; rather, it is the fundamentalist who over decades has postured himself into a more entrenched and closed-minded position.

By this point the reader may be getting suspicious that this author espouses something other than a strict, young-earth creationist position. That is not the case. Panama Baptist Church teaches the young earth creation model,[12] though strictly speaking it is not upheld through the Articles of Faith,[13] and this author is personally committed to it.[14] The point is that without some vital and enduring confessional standard, any temporally-situated issue may be allowed to become another litmus test for fellowship among believers. What is primary becomes encrusted with what is secondary, or even tertiary in importance, and otherwise godly, like-minded believers begin to separate.

> Without some vital and enduring confessional standard, any temporally-situated issue may be allowed to become another litmus test for fellowship among believers.

Our fundamentalist forefathers left us an enduring legacy, which is nothing less than the preservation of evangelical Christian orthodoxy. That orthodoxy was once threatened by the spreading cancer of theological liberalism in our leading denominational seminaries and churches. Today, it is threatened by a brand of hyper-sectarianism that causes those not already associated with the fundamentalist camp to question whether there is any validity within it. It is viewed as hopelessly divided, and not without just cause. As a movement, fundamentalism has turned inward and grown increasingly suspicious of its own institutions and associations.

Of course, careful discernment will always be necessary to guard against encroaching heterodoxy. Heresy still rears up its head from time to time—every generation must confront it. But fundamentalists are no longer separating from the liberals and the neo-orthodox. They are separating from each other. They are separating from individuals and institutions which hold to and practice the same standards of belief. Where will it stop? Where *should* it stop? That is the subject of the next chapter.

Discussion Questions

1. Some say that if Christians are to be together in heaven one day, they should be able to come together in the present. Is that a valid argument? Why or why not?

2. How may a particular church benefit from cooperating with other churches? Are there disadvantages to inter-church cooperation?

3. What specific kinds of ministry may be open to churches that choose to associate or cooperate with other churches, that may not otherwise be available?

4. In your experience, what reasons have church leaders given for refusing to fellowship or cooperate with another church? Are those reasons valid?

5. In your view, what are some legitimate reasons that a church should refuse fellowship with another church or association of churches?

Chapter 7

Application to Inter-Church Ministry, Part 2

—ᘏᴠ—

—⟀—

N ear the end of the last chapter, we discussed the need of some vital and enduring confessional standard against which equally-committed Christians[1] could decide the level of cooperation they may practice with one another. To determine what those confessional standards ought to be, we must direct our inquiry back to the Scriptures. When we do that—when we address the separation question through the clarifying lens of Scripture—we find that, in contrast to the separation practiced by so many fundamentalists, the biblical warrant for the practice of ecclesiastical separation involves the presence of either of three things: an explicit *denial* of Christ (apostasy from the essentials of apostolic faith), open *disobedience* to Christ, or an attempted *division* of Christ.

Regarding defection from apostolic doctrine, David Nettleton has written, "Some things are not essential to salvation but they are essential to full obedience, and the Christian has no liberty under God to sort out the Scriptures into essentials and non-essentials."[2] Is Dr. Nettleton correct in what he writes, or have the apostles and their closest associates given us explicit guidelines for ascertaining what is essential to fellowship and cooperation? All Scripture is equally inspired, to be sure, but is one's understanding of every Scripture the possible ground for censure and isolation? That last question must be answered in the negative, as the following analysis of Scripture will prove.

Denial of Christ

The first of the biblical warrants for separating churches from each other involves an explicit denial of Christ. Writing to the Galatian believers, Paul writes in very certain terms concerning those false teachers who had promulgated a false gospel of works:

> I am astonished that you are so quickly deserting the one who called you by the grace of Christ and are turning to a different gospel—which is really no gospel at all. Evidently some people are throwing you into confusion and are trying to pervert the gospel of Christ. But even if we or an angel from heaven should preach a gospel other than the one we preached to you, let him be eternally condemned! As we have already said, so now I say again: *If anybody is preaching to you a gospel other than what you accepted, let him be eternally condemned* (Gal 1:6-9).

Perhaps it is not asking too much to assume that no cooperative ministry should continue with those for whom Paul has declared the greatest condemnation. But Paul does not condemn those who err on secondary doctrinal points, those among whom the essential truths of the Gospel are shared with conviction. Rather, he condemns those who preach an entirely *different* gospel, one stemming from the Law and not from Grace.

The Apostle John also writes about the false teachers who had already begun to infiltrate the church:

> Many deceivers, who do not acknowledge Jesus Christ as coming in the flesh, have gone out into the world. Any such person is the deceiver and the antichrist. Watch out that you do not lose what you have worked for, but that you may be rewarded fully. Anyone who runs ahead and does not continue in the teaching of Christ does not have God; whoever continues in the teaching has both the Father and the

Son. *If anyone comes to you and does not bring this teaching, do not take him into your house or welcome him. Anyone who welcomes him shares in his wicked work* (2 John 7-11).

Here it is clear that John refers to flagrant apostates who actually deny the reality of God's incarnation in Christ. John does not advocate any unnecessary divisions within the body of Christ. Then there is the exhortation from Jude:

Dear friends, although I was very eager to write to you about the salvation we share, I felt I had to write and urge you to contend for the faith that was once for all entrusted to the saints. For certain men whose condemnation was written about long ago have secretly slipped in among you. They are godless men, who change the grace of our God into a license for immorality *and deny Jesus Christ our only Sovereign and Lord* (Jude 1:3-4).

Here again, Jude is not arguing for the severing of ecclesiastical ties between those godly men and women in our day who disagree on the length of creation days or the precise timing of Christ's rapture for the church, nor even the proper mode of baptism. Rather, he insists upon discriminating among those who understand and practice the pure Gospel of Grace, and those who demonstrate ignorance of that Gospel and who deny the Lord Jesus Christ by their actions. If the Galatian error was legalism, then the more general error in the churches was antinomianism, a licentious perversion of the Gospel of Grace. Such strong words and their attendant response as given by Jude are for Christians to use against apostate teachers, not for orthodox Baptists, Presbyterians, and Methodists to use against each other.

This is precisely the position held by a few prominent fundamentalists ministering outside of groups like the GARBC. John R. Rice was adamant about a believer's refusing to "yoke up" in ministry together with unbelieving infidels (i.e., liberals), but he was equally adamant about believers being able to cooperate with other believers. According to Rice, a believer may stay wherever he "can preach the whole truth, can support only what he ought to support, can oppose anything he ought to oppose and maintain his place as a called preacher of God, subject to Christ. . . ."[3] Rice removed himself from the Southern Baptist Convention because of the growing liberal presence there, but he continued to cooperate with Bible-believing Southern Baptists who stayed in. He viewed the Scriptures as teaching primary, but not secondary, separation. He would cooperate with anyone who was "for Christ and the Bible." That cooperation included members of other denominations, even some who themselves had "fellowship with some who fellowship with some they ought not fellowship with."[4]

The late Francis Schaeffer is another prominent conservative who held to this position. He was adamant that there was no "separation" in Christ, that is, among true Christians:

> But in a day like ours, let us recognize the proper hierarchy of things. The real chasm is not between the Presbyterians and everybody else, or the Lutherans and everybody else, or the Anglicans and everybody else, or the Baptists and everybody else, etc. The real chasm is between those who have bowed to the living God and thus also to the verbal, propositional communication of God's Word, the Scriptures, and those who have not.[5]

In summary, to answer the nettlesome question of whether we ever have a duty to separate what is essential from what is non-essential, the answer is "Yes." That affirmation stems not only from a study of biblical passages related to separation, but from our previous study of Paul's declaration in 1 Corinthians 15 concerning those things that were "of first importance." But before leaving this question, we should examine one other practical example of how that principle was practiced in apostolic times. One of the great truths of which all believers ought to be convinced is the liberty we have in Christ, our freedom from bondage to the Law. That is a part of what Christ purchased for us. The fact is, however, Paul "compromised" this truth. He knew what was true of himself in Christ. Nevertheless, he chose not to live his position and privilege in Christ before certain believers, *just so* he might continue to have a ministry among them (and with them).

Paul's explanation for his exemplary behavior is given in two well-known passages, 1 Corinthians 8 and Romans 14. In these two passages, Paul explains the need for a strong believer to live in such a way that the weaker brother is not offended and made to stumble. In a very practical way, Paul suppresses what he knows to be true; he chooses not to live outwardly what is true of himself inwardly, for by doing so he will have failed to minister the truth in love. More to our point, he will have forfeited his ministry among the Corinthians. It would seem that Paul was given liberty just so he might learn to control it and coexist without it. In this case, at least, it would appear that we are given *truth*, just so we might *hold it in* and guard it, especially where that truth might unnecessarily offend another brother, "for whom Christ died" (1 Cor 8:11). On doctrinal issues, only those views which would deny the Person and salvific work of the Lord Jesus Christ, as delineated through the course of our study in Acts and the various Epistles, would disqualify churches from at least limited joint fellowship or ministry.

> On doctrinal issues, only those views which would deny the Person and salvific work of the Lord Jesus Christ . . . would disqualify churches from at least limited joint fellowship or ministry.

Disobedience of Christ

Another valid reason for separating churches involves the area of obedience. If the first valid basis for separation concerned a church's *confession*, the second concerns a church's *conduct*. The one has to do with *profession*, the other with *practice*. Paul writes:

> In the name of the Lord Jesus Christ, we command
> you, brothers, to *keep away* from every brother who
> is idle and does not live according to the teaching
> you received from us. . . . We hear that some among
> you are idle. They are not busy; they are busybodies.
> Such people we command and urge in the Lord Jesus
> Christ to settle down and earn the bread they eat. And
> as for you, brothers, never tire of doing what is right.
> If anyone does not obey our instruction in this letter,
> take special note of him. *Do not associate with him,*
> in order that he may feel ashamed. Yet do not regard
> him as an enemy, but warn him as a brother (2 Thess
> 3:6-15).

Paul writes about the need to separate an individual believer
from the assembly when that believer "does not live according to the
teaching." His walk does not conform to the transformational truth
concerning Christ which he has heard and purported to believe. So
Paul is not writing about the need to separate churches from other
churches upon that basis. Still, perhaps an application may be made
for churches in an analogous situation. Take, for example, a church
that, while professing orthodoxy in its official documents or liturgy,
does not believe nor practice that orthodoxy. Another church may find
it necessary to break fellowship with the offending church precisely
because it does not conduct itself "according to the teaching." It
does not conform to the truth, although it may still confess the truth.
Much of what goes by the "liberal" label ought really to be categorized under the heading of "dead orthodoxy." After all, what mainline Presbyterian church in good standing does not at least officially
stand by the Westminster Confession? To improvise on Pickering's
words, apostasy must be defined not in terms of what the apostate
professes to believe, but in terms of what they actually do.

Paul has a similar exhortation for Timothy. If the Majority Text[6]
be allowed to stand, then the Apostle Paul establishes the proper
ground for separating from another professing Christian worker
when he writes:

> If anyone teaches false doctrines and does not agree
> to the sound instruction of our Lord Jesus Christ and
> to godly teaching, he is conceited and understands
> nothing. He has an unhealthy interest in controversies
> and quarrels about words that result in envy, strife,
> malicious talk, evil suspicions and constant friction
> between men of corrupt mind, who have been robbed
> of the truth and who think that godliness is a means
> to financial gain. *From such withdraw yourself*
> (1 Tim 6:3-5, Majority Text).

Whatever the threshold below which a teaching is determined to
be "false," both the extended and immediate context in which this
command occurs may suggest that the primary determinant is the
canon of one's personal morality. False teaching and moral laxity
often go hand in hand, and Paul commands that Timothy reject the
kind of teaching that leads to godlessness. So-called evangelical
churches that promote some form of prosperity gospel, for example,
are probably poor candidates for evangelistic cooperation. Godless
gain and the true Gospel do not make good co-belligerents on the
mission field. Paul gives a similar exhortation to Timothy in his
second letter:

> But mark this: There will be terrible times in the last
> days. People will be lovers of themselves, lovers of
> money, boastful, proud, abusive, disobedient to their
> parents, ungrateful, unholy, without love, unfor-
> giving, slanderous, without self-control, brutal, not
> lovers of the good, treacherous, rash, conceited,
> lovers of pleasure rather than lovers of God—having
> a form of godliness but denying its power. *Have
> nothing to do with them* (2 Tim 3:1-5).

Here again, those whom Paul earmarks for dismissal are those
whose profession is perhaps even orthodox, but whose practice of personal morality is severely lacking. The word Paul uses
is *morphōsis*, having the outward form or appearance of being

genuinely Christian, yet inwardly lacking its reality. A severance of fellowship is warranted when an individual or group *professes* the truth but does not *possess* the truth. Lip service to the Gospel and actual fidelity to the Gospel are two different things altogether.

Many "secondary" separationists[7] in our day abuse these passages dealing with disobedience to exclude from fellowship any believer that is not "obedient" on matters, say, of believer's baptism or immersion—the kinds of distinctive practice that historically have served to denominate our churches. Rather than to view these practices as a difference in biblical understanding, secondary separationists choose to assume that they evidence a willful lack of commitment to Scripture. Methodist, Congregational, Presbyterian, and Baptist churches that once cooperated on some limited basis under control of the Classic Fundamentalists[8] are made to exist in totally separate spheres under the ruling class in fundamentalist churches today. In every scriptural instance, however, the basis for removal of fellowship was a moral and ethical breach of behavior that would discredit the clear testimony of Christ.

Division of Christ

The final reason for separating from another church is when that church has already displayed its own spiritual arrogance and disaffection with the larger Body of Christ. In this case, there is apparently no need to expend undue energy attempting to woe that church back into a larger evangelical fellowship. Timothy George has noted correctly that Christian unity ought not to be pursued at the expense of moral purity, theological integrity, nor even genuine diversity.[9] We have addressed his first two points already. His third point fits nicely here. Those who would impose a far more limited understanding of Christian unity—one that depends for its existence upon complete uniformity—may be charged with inciting unnecessary division.

Again, Paul writes to a more personal situation, but the principle involved remains the same: "I urge you, brothers, to watch out for those who cause divisions and put obstacles in your way that are contrary to the teaching you have learned. *Keep away from them*" (Rom 16:17). Paul addresses the apostolic teaching already received, but he also touches upon their toleration of those who promote divisions within the assembly. In our day, this error can be seen on an ecclesiastical level in those denominations that are inclusivist in orientation. Evangelicals in those denominations permit the presence of theological liberals,[10] and therefore those denominations are continually embroiled in disputes over doctrinal and moral standards.

Finally, Paul addresses Titus with the following exhortation:

> But avoid foolish controversies and genealogies and arguments and quarrels about the law, because these are unprofitable and useless. Warn a divisive person once, and then warn him a second time. After that, have nothing to do with him (Titus 3:9-10).

Here is the false division erected by the secondary-separationist. Any theological controversy is made the pretext for disunion. Any variance in practice is made the grounds for separation. Outside of those controversies that threaten to undermine what is core, apostolic, essential Christian faith, such wrangling is "unprofitable and useless." Those who have been exposed to the more extreme wing of the King James Only movement have experienced first-hand how a baseless controversy can wreck churches and divide believers.[11] In this unending contest, some choose to take captive the scriptural doctrine of Preservation so that the pure Word of God can only be preserved in the King James Version of the Bible. No other translation, however literal and whatever its textual pedigree, can supplant the "Authorized" KJV without having violated the Preservation principle.

The biblicist is one who gladly cooperates with any group or individual that believes and proclaims that Jesus Christ is Lord and Savior, that He offers forgiveness from sin by His dying and rising from the dead, and that by believing in Christ we are forgiven.

So whereas the new evangelical error is in cooperating with the theological liberal, the fundamentalist error is in cooperating with scarcely anyone. The biblicist is one who gladly cooperates with any group or individual that believes and proclaims that Jesus Christ is Lord and Savior, that He offers forgiveness from sin by His dying and rising from the dead, and that by believing in Christ we are forgiven—Christ, Cross, and Conversion. The biblicist has an unqualified affinity with those who believe that eternal life is found only in the response of faith to God's saving initiative in Christ, a repentant faith in Jesus Christ as Lord and Savior, an owning up to one's own sinfulness and a willful trusting that what God did by Jesus Christ is sufficient to save us. The biblicist will work together with those who affirm by word and testimony that these things are true, and he will separate from those professed Christians who do not.

Noted pastor and author Chuck Swindoll understands all too well the fundamentalist mindset—it once was his own:

> There was a time in my life when I had answers to questions no one was asking. I had a position that was so rigid I would fight for every jot and tittle. I mean, I couldn't list enough things that I'd die for. The older I get, the shorter that list gets, frankly.[12]

Chuck Swindoll awakened to his ungracious spirit. To be sure, he still adheres to a pretribulational Rapture and a moderate Calvinism in his teaching, and by no means can he be labeled a Pentecostal. But he extends at least limited fellowship toward those Reformed and Pentecostal believers with whom he strenuously disagrees. That is a mark of grace, and that is precisely the character which God desires in each of us as we hold forth the truth in love.

Discussion Questions

1. Is it true that we should separate essential from non-essential doctrine before deciding with whom and to what extent we fellowship? Are you doing that now?

2. Chuck Swindoll confesses to have shortened his list of "essentials" over time. Are you willing to reexamine the list of things that you are "willing to die for"?

3. Assuming that you belong to a church which practices believer's baptism, do other churches that practice infant baptism evidence a *misunderstanding* of Scripture or *disobedience* to Scripture? How does your answer affect your ability to associate with those churches?

4. The author cited the "King James Only" controversy as something that unnecessarily divides churches. What other issues divide Bible-believing churches? Are those valid issues over which to deny fellowship?

5. How have your views on separation changed over time? Are you presently open to reexamining your assumptions and conclusions on this important issue?

Chapter 8

A Practical Guide to Cooperative Ministry

—ɯ—

W e spent quite a bit of space in the last chapter laying out certain conditions under which separating from other professed Christian individuals or organizations would appear to be necessary. Among those excluded from any level of cooperative fellowship were those who are in *denial* of the Person of Christ or His salvific work, those who are openly *disobedient* (and unrepentant) concerning a clear moral precept of Scripture, or those who themselves are the cause of unnecessary *division* in the body of Christ. Our alliterated list of criteria was easy to remember and recite, and it probably would have preached well, but it does leave us with some important questions when it comes time to actually apply those criteria to real-world situations. The last thing we want to do is leave the reader with vague theories but without any practical guidelines for use in ministry.

As an example of a real-world situation, Panama Baptist Church (PBC) had recently to grapple with whether or not it should continue participation in the community's annual Baccalaureate service for graduating seniors. The Panama Central School, while serving several townships, is located directly within the village of Panama. Everything — kindergarten through twelfth grade — is contained under one roof. As for the village itself, the 2000 Census lists just 491 residents living in 191 housing units, not counting seventeen other units that were vacant at the time. That eminently qualifies Panama for inclusion in the list of proverbial "map dots." When school is in session, the population of Panama triples in size. That kind of demographic data suggests that, to be considered active in the community, one had better be active in the school. There is not much else going on, except on Memorial Day and one Saturday before Christmas when Santa shows up at the only restaurant in town.[1] By now it should appear rather obvious that the question of whether to forego participation in the community Baccalaureate is not one that should be settled lightly.

Each year, the Baccalaureate is held in the local United Methodist church, over which there is strong evangelical leadership. Typically, Roman Catholic and various Protestant clergy also participate in this exercise on the invitation of students in their congregations. Most of the Protestant clergy, whether mainline or otherwise, would identify themselves as evangelical as to their personal faith commitments, while some are expressly liturgical.[2] Without question, the Baccalaureate looks and behaves like a worship service — there are readings from Scripture, several prayers, sacred music selections, even a short sermon. Occasionally, select students will give verbal testimony to their Christian faith. Can an independent Baptist church make the case for participating in an event such as this, if only to maintain some standing in the community and earn the right to be heard?

If what has just been described were a complete description of these community events, our decision would be relatively easy. We would participate (and we have) though perhaps not without a small bit of discomfort. But now comes the real tight spot. With a growing Mormon presence in our area, we have had representatives of that movement participating on the platform with increasing regularity. They pray or read Scripture along with the rest of us. That development raises some new questions. By continuing with our participation, have we ventured, albeit passively, into syncretistic worship? After all, are we not working hand in hand with representatives of a movement that explicitly denies the unique divinity of Jesus and the sufficiency of His blood? How can participation in worship with one or more leaders of a theological cult possibly be honoring to God? More than all that, how much theological confusion are we sowing among those who watch and listen? On the flip side, do we stand to generate even more misunderstanding within our tight-knit community by staying away?

Life can quickly become complicated. In response to questions like these, our associate pastor and I have spent some time putting together a short document entitled "Pastoral Policy on Christian Cooperation." While not a part of our Constitution or Bylaws, this policy does govern when it is appropriate for Panama Baptist Church to cooperate with an outside group in the planning and staging of an event or any other initiative that has an overriding religious purpose or orientation. Before getting into the substance of that document, it must be said that any particular initiative may warrant a stricter stance than what the policy requires. Moreover, it must be emphasized that this policy does not govern purely civic or political activities. Participation in a Memorial Day observance at the local cemetery, for example, is not addressed by our policy.

The document addresses the question of Christian cooperation on three different levels. A complete description of those levels is given below in the hope that it may serve as a model for other churches, whether or not they choose to adopt it in all the details. The point is that every church should think through these issues scripturally with a view towards defining and maintaining a consistent practice of biblical separation. Without set boundaries, the tendency on the part of churches is either to err on the side of caution and do nothing with other groups, or to do just about anything with little thought to the potential consequences.

> Without set boundaries, the tendency on the part of churches is either to err on the side of caution and do nothing with other groups, or to do just about anything.

Controlling Presence

We have labeled our first level of cooperation as that for which PBC has a *controlling* presence. An initiative for which PBC has a controlling presence is one in which we have sole or joint sponsorship. The practical test is simple. If PBC were to fail to deliver on its obligations, the initiative could reasonably be expected to fail. For such initiatives, all joint sponsors must subscribe to Article III of the PBC Constitution without mental reservation. That is the section of our Constitution which spells out our views on biblical inerrancy and the essential doctrines of God, Christ, Man, Sin, and Salvation.[3] Practically speaking, joint sponsors must be of Baptist or Protestant Evangelical conviction. In the Baccalaureate example we have been considering, PBC does not have a controlling presence. Our absence would be noticed, but the show would go on. Therefore, this section of our policy does not even apply.

In case that sounds altogether too dismissive by some, it should be noted that it is precisely here we stop short of a more inclusive position perhaps best represented by the well-known evangelist Billy Graham. Over a period of several decades, Graham has come to practice a rather extreme brand of ecumenical evangelism through his personal crusades, cooperating with Roman Catholic and Protestant clergy with little or no concern for theological pedigree or proven commitment to the biblical Gospel. Billy Graham writes, "We were determined to cooperate with all who would cooperate with us in the public proclamation of the Gospel. . . ."[4] Lest there be any misunderstanding on this point, Graham made it clear that he could cooperate even with those who did not necessarily share his views concerning Christ, nor even the Gospel: "Our message was clear, and if someone with a radically different theological view somehow decided to join with us in a Crusade that proclaimed Christ as the way of salvation, he or she was the one who was compromising personal convictions, not we."[5] Our first level of cooperation precludes such practice on the part of PBC. For us, cooperation at that level is to afford aid and comfort—even an explicit endorsement—to the enemies of Christ who parade as wolves in sheep's clothing *while on our turf and under our watch.*

Cooperative Presence

We labeled our second level of cooperation as that for which PBC has a *cooperative* presence. An initiative for which we have a cooperative presence is one in which we have some kind of leadership or facilitative role. We are not the prime movers, but we have agreed to take a fairly visible role. The practical test is again rather straightforward. If PBC were to fail to deliver on its obligations in this instance, the initiative, while affected, could reasonably be expected to succeed. For such an initiative, we determined that all facilitators must be historically "Christian." That is, the initiative must not be openly syncretistic. Practically speaking, facilitators must be historically orthodox in their Christian affiliation (e.g., Catholic, Orthodox, or Protestant). This excludes any member of the theological cults (e.g., Mormons, Jehovah's Witnesses, or practitioners of Christian Science).

An example of an initiative for which PBC has had a cooperative presence is precisely the community Baccalaureate service. Under these policy guidelines, we determined that our participation in future Baccalaureates either must be selective or at least well-understood. By "selective," we mean that our participation has to be conditioned upon there being no members of the theological "Christian" cults, or members of any other false religious system (e.g., Buddhists or Muslims) on the platform. By "well-understood," we mean that everyone in the audience should be made at least to recognize that the Baccalaureate is *not* a joint worship service, all appearances to the contrary. We constructed a disclaimer to that effect:

> While each of us on the platform are agreed upon the need for a personal relationship with God, we may not all agree as to who God is, nor how to have that relationship with Him. We are gathered for one purpose—to honor you, the PCS Class of 2006.

We were not gathered to worship God in any formal sense; rather, we were gathered to recognize our graduating seniors. Once we had constructed a paradigm for decision-making, our course of action became considerably more clear.

Consumer Presence

Our third level of cooperation is that for which PBC has a *consumer* presence. An initiative for which PBC has a consumer presence is one in which we merely participate. The practical test is again clear-cut. If PBC were to fail to "show up," there is absolutely no impact to the program. The show would go on and we would hardly be missed, except perhaps by some who for one reason or another *expected* us to show up. As a preservative measure, such initiatives must not openly violate our own group conscience with respect to doctrine or practice. For example, whereas PBC may participate in a gathering at which, say, Pentecostals may be present, there must not be a Pentecostal emphasis in public worship. The annual See You At the Pole (SYATP) rallies, for which Christian students gather around their school's flagpole for prayer at the beginning of the day, is a good example of something for which we have a consumer presence and gladly participate as a visible demonstration of Christian unity.

Christians of all theological persuasions must resist the urge to undervalue and retreat from that kind of visible, demonstrable unity. Jesus prayed concerning His followers, "May they be brought to complete unity *to let the world know that you sent me*" (John 17:23). On the basis of this verse, Francis Schaeffer has sounded a shrill but necessary warning: "Jesus gives the world the right to judge whether the Father has sent the Son on the basis of whether the world sees observable love among all true Christians."[6] At minimum a consumer presence, if not a cooperative presence, is necessary because the preservation of visible unity is at least as important as the protection of vital doctrine. One does not trump the other. God's directive is "both-and" rather than "either-or."

Again, the purpose in presenting this policy on Christian cooperation is not so that everyone adopts the same set of guidelines for use in their own church. Rather, it is shared in the expectation that believers in leadership positions will be challenged and encouraged to think through their own position (or lack thereof), and begin to formulate a policy for themselves that is both honoring to Scripture and workable in the details. No longer can churches "play it safe." Instead, churches must work within a set of cooperative guidelines that will preserve a clear biblical testimony, and yet leave doors open to both institutional and personal ministry.

A failure to approach the matter of separation in this manner, and with the kind of grace embraced by Chuck Swindoll in the previous chapter, leads at last to the worst kind of innuendo, name-calling, and back-stabbing. Those whose practice of separation is most immoderate do great harm to the cause of Christ, causing needless strife and division. The following extended tirade by George Dollar, a self-avowed "militant" fundamentalist writing in the 1970s, demonstrates the tremendous lengths to which some will go in order to discredit faithful, articulate, albeit imperfect, ministers of the Gospel:

> Those whose practice of separation is most immoderate do great harm to the cause of Christ, causing needless strife and division.

> Should Fundamentalists cooperate with those who cooperate in inclusivist ministries and meetings? Should a Fundamentalist cooperate with a leader like John Walvoord of Dallas Seminary, who for ten years has brought non-Fundamentalists to speak at Dallas? Should Fundamentalists cooperate with a pastor like J. Vernon McGee, who cooperated with Bishop Kennedy in the Graham Los Angeles campaign? Should Fundamentalists endorse a man like W. A. Criswell of First Baptist Church in Dallas as long as he supports the Cooperative Program of the Southern Baptist Convention. . . ? Should Fundamentalists continue to support Moody Bible Institute, whose president, George Sweeting, supported a Graham Crusade in Chicago? . . . Are these men mentioned above not a part of an unorganized movement, which, for want of any official recognition or name, we may refer to as the SSS (Silence, Sympathy, or Support)?[7]

Perhaps you recognize some of the leading lights singled out for rebuke by Dollar—Walvoord, McGee, Criswell, Sweeting. Perhaps it can be said that it is fortunate at least some of the persons named by Dollar have been promoted to glory, to a place where they no longer have to bear with the insults of "fellow" ministers, and where at last they have heard those welcome words, "Well done, thou good and faithful servant." Who is *not* on the militant's black list? At what point in ministry will a "misstep" land one's name on the "naughty" list of some self-appointed and published Protestant pope? By all means we should adopt a consistent practice of biblical separation, keeping far away from those who deny Gospel truth and deceive the lost under the guise of Christian ministry, but we must season that practice with grace, especially as we relate to other godly ministers who draw the lines a bit differently.

John R. Rice drives this same point home in his own whimsical way:

> If you are going to have secondary separation, then you must separate from everybody who doesn't separate from his grandmother and separate from his uncle and separate from his good friends. If you do not put your separation on the Bible basis of separation . . . of believers from unbelievers, then there is not any end to the separation. If you separate from everybody except those who are absolutely perfect in obedience, then, of course, you have no one but the superstar of all orthodoxy, yourself, with whom you can have fellowship![8]

Rice observes in another place, "One who believes in secondary separation finds he must also believe in tertiary separation."[9] He is correct in noting that there really is no logical end to the division once a person decides to exceed the biblical standard.

Francis Schaeffer describes the militant fundamentalist perfectly: "Those who come out tend to become hard; they tend to become absolutists even in the lesser points of doctrine."[10] The harshness and stridency once visited upon Bible-denying apostates is directed with equal force at the Christian who happens to hold a differing point of view on some non-essential matter. No practical distinction is made between the believer who disagrees and the unbelieving infidel who misleads. In contrast to that kind of combatant and unbiblical attitude, Schaeffer rightly affirms that one can believe in absolutes without adopting an "absolutist mentality" over everything. He correctly maintains that "the Christian doctrinal and intellectual position lays down a circle rather than a point. . . . We should see the edge of the circle as an absolute limit past which we 'fall off the edge of the cliff' and are no longer Christians at this particular point in our thinking."[11] Within that circle of orthodoxy, Christians can and should fellowship with one another, affording the world a visible demonstration of unity even as they disagree on lesser things.

Incidentally, George Dollar makes clear the reason for his vitriol when finally he asks, "Since [these men] will not take a militant stand against all forms of compromise and middle-of-the roadism . . . are they not causing further erosion of historic Fundamentalism?" Perhaps he was being more candid than he knew. At some point in their careers, men like Dollar ceased giving themselves to the articulate defense and proclamation of a Person, and instead gave themselves to the defense of a movement. That movement, called Fundamentalism, is but a tiny blip on the current church scene, as well as upon the whole sweep of church history. Some, at least, have given their lives to ensuring that it survives, if only in small pockets, and they do so whatever the collateral damage to godly and equally committed servants of Christ.

Discussion Questions

1. What are your church's stated policies on cooperative ministry? You may want to speak with your pastor or church leader for help with your answer.

2. In what inter-church or community events does your church participate? Do you know of events that your church purposefully avoids?

3. Are you in agreement with the policy on cooperation presented in this chapter? What specific points, if any, would you change?

4. Is there a church in your area that you or your church would consider to be overly inclusive in terms of the extent of its cooperative ministry? Why?

5. If you are a pastor or church leader and your church does not presently have a well-defined policy on cooperative ministry, are you prepared to begin constructing one? How would you begin?

Chapter 9

Application to Intra-Church Ministry

While the primary stress in the previous few chapters was on applying an understanding of what is essential to Christian faith toward cooperative inter-church ministry, an equally valid application may be made toward *intra*-church ministry—that is, to what goes on *within* a particular local church. If certain clear truths of Scripture are essential and non-negotiable, while other (perhaps less clear) truths are non-essential and of lesser importance, then perhaps the very structure of our doctrinal statements and our use of those doctrines in church life require scrutiny. For example, must an adult believer be required to affirm every part of a church's doctrinal statement before becoming a member? The answer to that question likely depends upon what membership "buys" you. If membership confers the right to teach in the Sunday School, then the answer may be "Yes," on the ground that teaching throughout a church's educational program ought to be consistent with its formal confession. If ministry qualifications are decided upon some other basis, however, then the answer may well be "No."[1]

The stickier issue is related to the fact that membership normally confers upon an individual the right to vote in a congregational business meeting, assuming that a church is at least nominally congregational in polity. One may argue that members with voting rights ought definitely to agree with every part of the church's doctrine; that hedge, after all, is what guarantees that the church's theological center will not drift over time. It is no wonder that some fundamental churches opt for that sort of an "easy fix," and err on the side of caution. To "join" these churches, one must indicate total agreement with the doctrinal position of the church, or least be seen as open and "teachable."[2] For the most part it would appear that such a strategy has worked, judging from the growth of fundamental churches in some circles. There is the perhaps well-deserved perception, however, that all these churches have succeeded in producing are entire congregations of uncritical dogmatists. They know *what* they believe, they have every article of belief locked down with a single proof text, and they generally are not willing to consider any alternatives. They are taught only to affirm, never to question.

A number of years ago I attended the adult Sunday School class of an independent Baptist church in McLean, Virginia. We had been discussing Christ's impeccability, and the instructor asked how it was that Christ, though perfectly human, could have been sinless. One student suggested that Christ was sinless because He had been conceived by the Holy Spirit. I proceeded to suggest that *perhaps* the sin nature may just as well have come down to Him through Mary, so that perhaps another explanation was in order. If you have never tried to raise an objection to the seminal theory of the spread of sin to the human race, and particularly in Baptist circles,[3] you may not be able to anticipate the reaction I received. Bear in mind, we were not debating the impeccability of Christ! One deacon immediately retorted, in a very abrupt manner meant to convey his authority, "Sin is transmitted through the male," effectively shutting down what would have been a delicious theological discussion. If this deacon is right, I expect that when we finally have gotten the courage to clone a human being, say, from a female of the species, we will have succeeded in producing a sinless individual. (But I digress.)

A more basic question must be answered, however: is there no room for theological diversity and discourse within a local assembly? Must the local body be theologically homogeneous? Indeed, can such a theological disposition be assumed in any church of significant size? While it may well be the case that we have suppressed legitimate biblical inquiry and short-circuited some much-needed and spirited theological discussion by such policies, it is probably unlikely that we have achieved true theological homogeneity anyway. Think of it this way: if all the members of a church *already* agree with one another on every point of understanding, then why not disband the adult Sunday School?

Aside from the theological inbreeding such an approach may engender, dealing with non-essential differences by suppressing them also requires a great deal more conformity than the apostles apparently would want for full participation in an assembly. On a more practical level, with such an approach it is difficult to avoid making some believers into second-class citizens of the church, excluded as they are from full participation (e.g., membership) on the basis of dissenting from some non-essential doctrinal distinctive.

A strategy for preserving doctrinal integrity

Erring on the side of caution need not give way to wholesale doctrinal latitude, however. Just a small measure of creativity can assure that the doctrinal distinctives of a church are not allowed to erode over time, even while allowing for vigorous theological reflection among the membership. In order for a church to ensure that it is able to preserve its own doctrinal heritage, it must do so at the level of the membership, the leadership, and the articles of faith.

Bounding the membership. First, *every* member ought to be required to affirm the essentials of Christian faith, profess a born again, saving experience, and submit to baptism. At the Panama Baptist Church, we assure these things as much as is humanly possible by having the member candidate meet with a pastor or deacon on two successive occasions. The first meeting is devoted entirely to that individual's testimony of conversion and baptism. We are unhurried in the way we probe a person's understanding of repentance and faith. As much as is humanly possible, we ensure that a person is in *possession* of salvation and not just in *profession* of salvation. We are concerned at least as much with whether a person demonstrates evidence of salvation in the present as with whether he or she has "made a decision" in the past.[4]

As for baptism, we ensure that a person understands what it means—that it pictures the historical death, burial, and resurrection of Christ; that it publicly identifies that individual with Christ in His death to sin and resurrection to life (Rom 6:1-4); that it serves as a declaration of faith and a public commitment to follow Christ, in that baptism is the first public act of obedience to Christ following salvation as directed by Scripture (Acts 2:41); and that it signals that individual's entrance into the visible church, much like Spirit baptism marked his entrance into the church universal (1 Cor 12:13).[5] In other words, we ensure the baptismal candidate knows what he is getting into. He knows what it means, has counted the cost, and is willing to proceed on that basis.

In our second meeting, we review the essentials of our faith, requiring complete agreement without mental reservation on such matters as biblical authority, the nature of God, the deity of Christ, the reality of sin, and the basis and means of salvation. We then review our distinctive doctrine, requiring that an individual conform to it by living (and teaching) in a manner that is in sympathy and consistent with it, and by agreeing not to campaign or agitate against it except to direct concerns toward a pastor or a deacon. Any deviation from that agreement is understood to be grounds for dismissal from the membership. Here we include our views on such issues as eternal security, spiritual gifts, and the Rapture. Formally separating that which is essential from that which is distinctive within the articles of faith is an issue we take up later in this chapter.

Also in our second meeting, we share what it means to be a member of our church and living in covenant community with other believers.[6] We review the covenant itself, the accepted method of conflict resolution, disciplinary procedures, and the conditions under which a person may request to be removed from the membership role. The candidate then makes a brief appearance before the full board of deacons, together with the pastors, so that the pastors and deacons together have an opportunity to ensure that he is qualified to become a member of the church. Barring any difficulty, the individual is recommended by the deacons to the congregation for a vote on membership.

Bounding the leadership. Beyond what is required for basic membership, those who seek the office of pastor (elder) and deacon should be required to affirm without reservation every part of a church's doctrinal statement. That is, those who hold spiritual office in the church must give their unqualified support both to essential evangelical doctrine as well as to that which is distinctive to the belief system of the church. Holding office in the church is not a right; rather, it is a matter of great privilege. Therefore, this requirement is not an infringement upon one's free inquiry into matters of theology. In fact, there are many other ways to serve God through the church other than as pastor or deacon. As a very practical matter, insisting upon unity of doctrine at the level of church leadership guards against unnecessary disagreement, especially when some debate is already contentious on other grounds.

But more to the point, pastors (elders) and deacons are the guardians or custodians of a church's doctrinal heritage. It is their solemn duty to protect and uphold the teaching standards of the church. If a change is to be made to the articles of faith, it will come about first as a consensual decision of the leadership team followed by a vote of the church. It will not come about through any form of politicking, neither by any block of rank and file members nor by any segment of the leadership formed for that purpose. Any such posturing may properly be viewed as promoting disunity and lead to disciplinary action.

Binding the articles of faith. The final leg of a three-point strategy for doctrinal integrity within the reflective church is simple: for any matter before the assembly (assuming some degree of congregational rule) that impinges upon the doctrinal standards of the church, the usual two-thirds or three-fourths vote is required of the general membership, but a unanimous decision is required of the pastor(s) and deacons. It may not even be altogether unreasonable to require the same two-thirds or three-fourths acceptance by the members of the board, as long as members of the leadership team are Spirit-led men who can be trusted to live with the final decision. An individual leader holding the minority opinion may step down from office, but his manner of doing so will not reflect poorly on the rest of the board. In this way, the doctrinal distinctives are at least as well-guarded as was the case when the church required homogeneity among the entire membership, reformation in the area of doctrine is at least permissible, and unity is maintained.

Daniel Wallace, professor of New Testament Studies at Dallas Seminary, has suggested a "taxonomy of doctrine," citing especially the tendency on the part of dispensationalists to "major on the minors" as pretext for his proposal. Significantly, he makes this observation as a footnote to his exposition of Paul's admonition to Timothy regarding the need to "correctly handle the word of truth" (2 Tim 2:15). Wallace states, "It is imperative that we hold to a hierarchy of doctrines and place our Christology and soteriology in the center."[7] What Wallace calls for is that which the church requires, and which we have recommended. Naturally, if the pastor(s) and deacons of a church are genuinely committed to its doctrinal affirmations, the governing board will be careful to ensure that those theological distinctives are being addressed through its educational ministries. Doctrines are lost to a church — not by cooperating with other evangelical churches — but by a failure to teach doctrine.

> Doctrines are lost to a church—not by cooperating with other evangelical churches—but by a failure to teach doctrine.

A case study

What follows is a somewhat typical independent, evangelical church doctrinal statement. This statement is that of the Paw Paw Bible Church, Paw Paw, West Virginia, where I previously served as Pastor:

THE BIBLE. We believe the Bible as the verbally inspired Word of God, wholly without error in the original writings, our all-sufficient rule of faith and practice (2 Tim 3:16; 2 Pet 1:21).

GOD. We believe in one God eternally existing in three persons — the Father, the Son, and the Holy Spirit — and that these three are equal in every divine perfection (Deut 6:4; Matt 28:19).

JESUS CHRIST. We believe that the eternal Son of God became incarnate in the Lord Jesus Christ, being conceived of the Holy Spirit and born of the virgin Mary, and is true God and true man; that He lived a sinless life, gave Himself in death as a perfect substitutionary sacrifice for the sins of all men, arose bodily from the grave, and ascended into heaven (John 1:1, 14, 18; 1 Cor 15:3-4).

THE HOLY SPIRIT. We believe that the Holy Spirit regenerates, baptizes, indwells, and seals all believers in Christ immediately upon salvation; and that He empowers for service those who are yielded to Him (John 3:6; 1 Cor 6:19; 1 Cor 12:13; Eph 4:30; 5:18).

SPIRITUAL GIFTS. We believe that God has given to all believers a spiritual gift (or gifts); that speaking in tongues is not a necessary sign for the baptism or filling of the Holy Spirit; and that ultimate deliverance of the body from sickness or death awaits the consummation of our salvation in the resurrection (1 Cor 12:11; 13:8; Eph 4:11-12).

MAN. We believe that mankind was originally created in the image and likeness of God; that in Adam he fell through sin and thereby incurred spiritual death which is eternal separation from God; so that now all men are sinners, hopelessly sinful in themselves, apart from the grace of God (Gen 1:27; Rom 3:23; 5:12).

SALVATION. We believe that salvation is received by grace through faith alone in the Lord Jesus Christ, on the ground of His shed blood and altogether apart from works; and that all who believe in Christ are born again by the Holy Spirit and thereby become the children of God, possessing every spiritual blessing (John 1:12; Eph 2:8-9; Titus 3:5).

ETERNAL SECURITY. We believe that all who are truly born again are assured of salvation and will, by the grace of God, persevere and be kept saved forever (John 10:27-29; Rom 8:29; 1 John 5:13).

SANCTIFICATION. We believe that, in Christ, every believer secures a holy standing before God; that in experience the believer progressively grows in grace and into Christ-likeness by the power of the Holy Spirit; and that the believer will be fully perfected at the appearing of Christ, such that his state will conform to his standing (John 17:17; Eph 5:25-27; Heb 10:10).

CHRISTIAN LIFE AND MISSION. We believe that every believer is called to a holy life of service and testimony in the power of the Holy Spirit, which service includes the proclamation of the Gospel to the whole world; and that there is promised reward in heaven for faithfulness to such service (Matt 28: 18-19; John 12:25-26; 1 Pet 1:15-16).

SEPARATION. We believe that every believer should separate from worldly and sinful practices and associations; and that Bible-believing churches should separate themselves entirely from worldliness and religious apostasy (Rom 12:1-2; 2 Cor 6:14; 7:1; 2 John 9-11).

THE CHURCH. We believe that the Church is composed of all true believers baptized by the Holy Spirit into one body that is Christ's; and that the local church is an assembly of born-again, immersed believers who regularly gather for the purposes of worship, fellowship, administration of the ordinances, edification, discipline, and effective promotion of the work of Christ throughout the world (Acts 2:41-42; Eph 1:22; Heb 10:24-25).

ORDINANCES. We believe that believer's baptism and the Lord's Supper are the only ordinances of the church. We further believe in immersion as the mode of baptism, and in the memorial significance of the Lord's Supper (1 Cor 11:23-26).

DISPENSATIONS. We believe that dispensations are stewardships by which God administers His purpose on the earth through man under varying responsibilities; that three of these are the subject of extended revelation in Scripture: Mosaic law, the present dispensation of grace, and millennial kingdom (Eph 3:2-6; Col 1:25-27; Heb 7:18-19).

ANGELS. We believe that angels were originally created as sinless spirit beings, and that many continue in their holy state as ministers of God; that Satan and many other angels rebelled against God, and in their fallen state continue to oppose God and His work (Col 1:16; Eph 6:12; Jude 6).

THE SECOND COMING. We believe that the blessed hope of the imminent return of the Lord Jesus Christ for His Church, commonly called the Rapture, is to be followed in order by: the Tribulation, the Second Coming of Christ to the earth, and the millennial reign of Christ (1 Thess 4:13-18; Titus 2:13).

THE ETERNAL STATE. We believe in the bodily resurrection of all men, the saved to everlasting blessedness in the presence of God, and the unsaved to judgment and everlasting punishment (Matt 25:46; John 5:28-29; Acts 24:15).

What is important in this statement of faith is not the presence of separatist or dispensational elements. It stands to reason that some readers will take exception to these and other features of this particular statement—these are, after all, what is *distinctive* about Paw Paw Bible Church. Every evangelical who reads this document should, however, note with appreciation those features that are *essential* to making Paw Paw Bible Church decidedly biblical and evangelical, such as its teaching concerning the Trinity, Jesus Christ, His sin-atoning death and bodily resurrection, and salvation by faith alone. Under the proposal given above for a two-tiered doctrinal standard (one for members, another for pastors and deacons), the sample doctrinal statement might be divided into two sections. Alternatively, of course, those paragraphs deemed to belong to the "essential" category may simply be footnoted as such and explained in subsequent text:

Tier 1	Tier 2
God	The Bible
Jesus Christ	The Holy Spirit
Man	Spiritual Gifts
Salvation	Eternal Security
The Eternal State	Sanctification
	Christian Life and Mission
	Separation
	The Church
	Ordinances
	Dispensations
	Angels
	The Second Coming

The precise content of each tier is subject to discussion, even when framed by our study in core Christian commitments. For example one may choose to handle the first section, "The Bible," at the first or the second tier, depending upon whether the formal principle is seen as tightly coupled with the material principle (to borrow from Carson). In the other direction, the paragraph that treats the doctrine of Man is assumed to be necessary context for the following paragraph on "Salvation," so that both are included in Tier 1. Perhaps, as well, the section dealing with Christ's Second Coming can be partitioned into that which is considered essential to the teaching of Christ (i.e., Christ will return bodily) and that which is distinctive (i.e., His return is completed in two stages, preceding and following the Tribulation).

The point is, every area of doctrine ought not to be placed on an equal footing with every other area of doctrine. There are the those doctrines which may be viewed as essential to evangelical faith, and then there are those doctrines which may be viewed as distinctive to a particular church, and therefore which may vary from church to church. That is not to deny that these distinctives are cherished doctrines, nor that they are biblically based in some way, but rather that they are not the things over which Christians must break meaningful fellowship. In point of fact, these are normally the doctrines which have little to do with a church's biblical mission of evangelism and discipleship. Various teachings in Scripture differ in importance. In fact, the lesser teachings tend to be those which receive limited treatment in Scripture, invariably leading to different viewpoints among equally committed and qualified Christians.

> Unity is a means to an end, not the end itself. But by the same token, we ought not to minimize our areas of agreement and overindulge our differences.

As with most areas of life and thought, balance would appear to be the key. We dare not minimize our differences as church members in some misguided attempt to establish what makes us similar. After all, unity is a means to an end, not the end itself. But by the same token, we ought not to minimize our areas of agreement and overindulge our differences. The latter error would seem to be the more prevalent problem within the contemporary American fundamentalist movement. It is a significant problem, as well, in the way that it effectively shuts people out. For people on the inside, who somehow abide the narrow test of membership, such appeal to uniformity breeds an unhealthy dogmatism while at the same time it stifles spirited, biblical inquiry. In the end, the way to preserve doctrine is not to enforce it, but to teach it. That is what the next chapter is about and, of course, that is what churches should have been doing all along.

Discussion Questions

1. Does your church practice a "taxonomy of doctrine"? If not, what elements of your church's existing faith statement would you include in the first tier?

2. Is there place for theological diversity within a church on matters not essential to Christian faith? Is such diversity healthy to a church? Why or why not?

3. How important is it that a church preserve its doctrine? Are there occasions when a long-held doctrine should be allowed to change? Please explain.

4. The author presented a three-point strategy for preserving a church's doctrinal heritage. Is that strategy sufficient? What changes would you make when adapting it to your church?

5. In your experience, do most Christians know *why* they believe as they do, or do they simply accept as dogma what they have been taught? Explain the importance of knowing why we believe as we do.

Chapter 10

The Importance of Continued Indoctrination

—◊◊◊—

—〰—

After reading this far into the book, with all of its stress on the need to major upon essentials rather than non-essentials, one runs the very real risk of deciding that distinctive doctrines have no place whatsoever in the church. More than one evangelical church appears to have gone in that direction, at least if we are to judge by the signs we see in church lawns. Significant numbers of churches have intentionally surrendered their denominational labels. Some of these have effectively surrendered their theological distinctives, as well. I say "effectively" because, while those distinctives are still listed in a doctrinal statement somewhere, they are never taught or promoted from the pulpit. It seems that for many churches, the charge of sectarianism is considered the worst possible indictment they could receive.

For many churches, of course, a non-denominational label is used simply to attract visitors to the services. This can be a valid strategy for reaching the lost, say, in a specific neighborhood or geographic area, for which a denominational label serves as a "stone of offense" to keep neighbors away. These churches do promote their distinctive doctrines through their teaching ministries. For other churches, however, "non-denominational" has come to mean "least common denominator." Church-goers at these churches hear nothing about eternal security or divine election—either for or against—nor any talk of pre-, mid-, or post-tribulationism. For these churches, ministry is built upon the Nicene Creed with a little evangelical piety and conversionism thrown in for good measure. Open identification with any particular theological persuasion or historical

Christian movement is jettisoned in favor of a ministry focus which offends no one.

The importance of distinctive doctrine to church identity

But majoring on the essentials need not imply that we avoid the teaching of non-essentials. Think about it—if an independent church identifies itself as evangelical, then the Bible serves as its authoritative measure of what is true, and *what* the Bible teaches becomes the standard by which other creeds and opinions are tested. It simply will not suffice to restrict one's teaching to only those portions of Scripture which deal with essential matters or, to put it more cynically, to those matters over which card-carrying evangelicals could not possibly disagree. To simply retreat from the more difficult passages of Scripture demonstrates less, not more, reverence for the Sacred Text.

Instead, each church must remain faithful to Scripture as that body comprehends it. The fact that other churches may disagree over the understanding of any portion of Scripture has no relevant bearing upon what a particular church does with what it "knows." Indeed, it must act upon what it "knows," for whatever is not done in faith is sin (Rom 14:23). By way of example, and risking the charge of relativism, we maintain that it is much less a problem for a convinced Methodist to forego believer's baptism than for a person raised in a Baptist church. Since the Baptist church-goer has been taught a baptistic reading of Scripture as it relates to baptism, that person had better have a firm conviction that her church is wrong-headed to require it before deciding against it. Otherwise, for her it would be downright sinful to avoid it. By the same reasoning, for a Baptist church to downplay what is distinctive to its theological heritage (based upon its shared reading of Scripture) for the sake of, say, more ecumenical "openness," would be to invite doctrinal apathy into its ranks.

If an independent church is at all faithful to teach the "whole counsel of God," it will continue to rigorously define itself theologically by what it purports the Bible to teach. The fact is, any independent, evangelical church is inherently sectarian; it is a denomination unto itself. While it shares with other evangelical churches a core body of essential, biblical truth concerned primarily with Christ and the Gospel, it will invariably differ on any number of lesser, nonessential issues. *And that's O.K.* In fact, it is more than O.K., because a church must be true to Scripture as it has faithfully understood it. Again, to do any less would be to sin.

And that is where a problem arises. In spite of its differences with other churches, the independent, evangelical church has no seminaries under its control to which it may reliably delegate the responsibility of preserving and propagating its distinctive faith to future leaders. Nor is there an external creed to which it may passively subscribe. For this reason, a church having a desire to maintain its unique place on the religious landscape, if not to preserve its very existence as a distinct organization, must take upon itself the responsibility to pass on or *teach* what is distinctive about its doctrine. The independent, evangelical church *remains* distinctive in degree as it *catechizes* both present and future generations in what is distinctive about itself.

> If an independent church is at all faithful to teach the "whole counsel of God," it will continue to rigorously define itself theologically by what it purports the Bible to teach.

Of course, what is distinctive about a church must continue to be distinguished from what is essential to its being Christian. As we have learned, evangelical churches are generally agreed upon the essentials (i.e., *fundamentals*) of the Christian faith, by the very definition of what it means to be evangelical. Much of what is distinctive to an evangelical church is inherently *nonessential*. Now, using a word like "nonessential" to describe biblical doctrine may offend those who are somewhat to the right of the evangelical "center." To these, labeling something as "nonessential" is cause for concern because that term suggests that some things may be set aside. To these, "nonessential" implies "not important," or dispensable, so that no perceived teaching of Scripture should be labeled "nonessential."

In view of this perception, it should again be stressed that by categorizing certain things as nonessential, we are *not* thereby suggesting that those doctrines no longer need to be taught and defended within the church. In fact, the underlying thesis of this chapter is that the very opposite is true: the evangelical church, accepting the Bible as its sufficient and authoritative measure and norm of what is true, must be true to its own understanding of Scripture over a broad range of subjects. As part of its fidelity to that understanding, a church will want to inculcate its doctrinal heritage in those who choose to affiliate with the church. Education in doctrine is a necessary component of responsible ministry within the independent, evangelical church.

The importance of distinctive doctrine to orthodoxy

Someone has said, "Since we gather around Jesus . . . it is our center, not our boundaries, that matter." Having lived through a great deal of rancor among the churches in recent decades, that statement increasingly resonates with Christians. They are war-weary, tired of the theological battles, and ready to join in a Great Big Group Hug. "Heresy" no longer exists in their minds, because the very notion of heresy conjures up old images of witch hunts and multiplied church schisms. But in an article entitled "Why We Believe in Heresy," Thomas Oden responds: "A center without a circumference is a dot, nothing more. . . . The circle of faith cannot identify its center without recognizing its margins."[1] In a later publication, Oden suggests that a church without boundaries can neither have a "liturgical center" nor even remain a worshipping community.[2] Without a circumference to define the center, there no longer is a circle.

To put flesh on Oden's ideas, it may be helpful for us to return to that sentiment about gathering around Jesus, and how Jesus is all that really matters. What Jesus might that be? What's in a name? Aren't we justified in asking, *What Jesus do we believe in*? Jesus is God, but who or what is God? Jesus became a man, but what is Man? Jesus saved me, but saved from what? Jesus died for my sins, but what is sin? Jesus was "made a little lower than the angels," but what are angels? So whereas Jesus may be at the center of Christian belief, we are justified in asking, Who is Jesus? Even through a cursory examination of preliminary questions like these, it becomes easy to see how one's take on the boundary questions are precisely the things that shape or give definition to one's overall view of Jesus. You may gather around Jesus if you like, but you had better figure out what He looks like.

Figure 3 illustrates the way in which a wide-ranging study of theology is necessary to a right view of Christ. Apart from such an investigation into various theological issues, "Jesus" becomes no more than a name to which we may attach our varied notions of God.[3] Everyone may claim to worship Him, but everyone is worshipping someone different. When a group refuses to bound itself doctrinally, it cannot hope to come together doxologically. True worship must have as its foundation a strong biblical theology that is capable of expressing truth on several interrelated fronts, yielding an accurate, coherent view of the person Jesus Christ.

Figure 3. The Circumference Defining the Center.

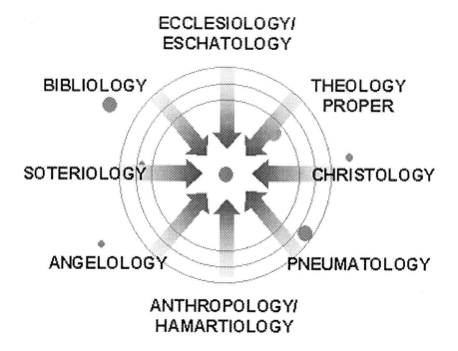

There are a myriad idols in the world that go by the name of "Jesus." As mentioned previously, the churches in our area help to lead up a community Baccalaureate service for our graduating seniors. By and large, it is led by evangelical ministers and one or more Roman Catholic clergymen. All are fairly orthodox, in a classical sense. However, if a Mormon student happens to be graduating, a Mormon clergyman is apt to be asked by that student to lead one of the many prayers during the service. What strikes me is that his words are thoroughly orthodox. In fact, he could teach some of the other ministers on the platform a thing or two about how to lead in a proper Trinitarian prayer. The only problem is that the Mormon minister is not Trinitarian. When it comes to his view of Jesus, he is heterodox, outside the pale of orthodoxy. He is helping to lead and grow a theological cult, and he is damning students to hell in the process.

To the Mormon, Jesus does not possess divinity in any unique sense. Instead, he is a pre-existent spirit like the rest of us, albeit the "firstborn." According to the Mormon minister, if the spiritual life is a race, then Jesus commands a respectable lead, but nothing more than that. That is to say, Jesus is different from other persons in degree, but not in kind. He is a god, but good Mormons may become gods also.[4] So while Mormonism does not have a monopoly on heresy, and the purpose of this section is not to single out Mormonism for criticism, our experience with the annual Baccalaureate does illustrate the need for theological precision among evangelical churches, especially within their circle of leadership. Card-carrying evangelicals ought to be theologically astute enough to be able to identify heresy when it walks in front of them.

Lest I am perceived at this point as being some far-right "fighting fundy," able to talk like an evangelical but forever bound to his fundamentalist heritage, let it be said that this concern for theological purity is precisely that raised by none other than Billy Graham during the 1950s, when the nascent World Council of Churches was beginning to rise in prominence. While Graham was generally accepting of attempts at ecumenical cooperation, still he feared "that in some circles . . . the preoccupation with unity was overshadowing a commitment to evangelism *and biblical theology*" (emphasis mine).[5] Billy Graham, dean of evangelicals, knew the importance of holding to biblical doctrine even as he worked towards a greater unity in the cause of evangelism.

The importance of indoctrination to the church

It stands to reason that if distinctive doctrine is important to a church, then it is critical for a church to *teach* doctrine. Much of contemporary teaching and preaching today, however, is geared so much toward the "felt needs" in the congregation as to minimize doctrinal instruction.[6] Few pastors would openly disparage the need of theological education, but the growth of theological illiteracy within so many churches would suggest that it is not happening—at least not well. If it does occur, it is not being done in a way that is getting desired results. In any case, the average person in the pew knows little of theology, nor does he care to know.[7]

That said, a disclaimer needs to be made. While it would appear that the need for doctrinal instruction within the church cannot be gainsaid, it is necessary to account for the many authoritarian, separatist churches that have endured over time with long-held doctrines firmly in place, even in the absence of a structured program of indoctrination. The characterization of these churches as both authoritarian and separatist is not without design. It is perhaps accurate to note that churches which evidence the greatest degree of authoritarianism or dogmatism are also the ones that engage the most rigid forms of separatism. These churches appear to succeed in large measure precisely *because* they have isolated themselves from the larger body of Christian churches, including even those that are self-consciously evangelical. For some, this observation is all the evidence that is needed to validate a more extreme brand of "secondary" separatism. Hopefully we have dealt sufficiently with that issue in previous chapters.

Of course, in a very real but pragmatic way, that arrangement has served well to preserve a fundamentalist heritage in many churches. The church that closes itself off from the wider body can afford a degree of laxity in genuine teaching. There simply is not a need to engage in a polemical defense of doctrinal distinctives if the membership is never challenged with competing beliefs. In a church that is closed off to other churches, dogmatic pronouncements are all that are needed. Among other maladies, however, such a church will never have opportunity to reform itself theologically, and its people will be more prone to develop unhealthy attitudes toward other believers and church groups. The importance of teaching becomes greater for the church that takes its proper place in the wider body of Christ. If believers belonging to a church are rightly encouraged to maintain a healthy openness toward believers who are affiliated with other evangelical traditions, they will necessarily come under the influence of teaching in nonessential areas that are opposed to the teaching norms of their own church.

Any believer who is reasonably grounded in doctrine and who listens to some of the teaching programs that are available on Christian radio, or who periodically browses a religious bookstore, is acutely aware of how many different doctrinal perspectives are accessible through the broadcast and print media. For example, much of the "triumphalism" and dominion[8] emphases being promulgated by popular radio speakers today are rooted in doctrinal perspectives that are antithetical to the Dispensational perspective of Panama Baptist Church, where I serve as pastor. Thus, a believer who is not well-grounded in the particular doctrinal perspective of PBC may wind up fairly confused by the many conflicting ideas being promoted by various radio and television programs or books. He runs the risk of having his mind become stuck in a sort of theological no-man's land, where competing ideas are made to coexist without coherency. If association is to be had without amalgamation, then theological education within the independent, evangelical church becomes even more critically important.

In view of the need to maintain and promulgate the particular doctrinal perspectives of a church, and in view of the cacophony of competing voices that exist today in the theological marketplace, we are now prepared to address the question that many seem to be asking: In the face of so many sources of variant teaching, can a pastor or teacher lead his church toward a more open fellowship with other evangelical believers, yet at the same time adequately present his flock with the broader theological stance of the church in such a way that it is not only understood, but properly *differentiated* from and *defended* against the many different theological positions to which a believer will become exposed? Practically, can a church seek fellowship on the basis of shared, essential doctrine, while maintaining (even strengthening) among its own people what is distinctive about itself?

Many fundamentalists flatly deny that such an arrangement is feasible. To these, a church which attempts fellowship with another church "of a different stripe" is destined for doctrinal compromise. Other (usually left-of-center) evangelicals are equally resolute in their denial that the attempt is either necessary or desirable; they say that the church should acquiesce to a least-common-denominator, essentialist mode of ministry—that such a ministry is the price to be paid in order to pursue more open relationships with other evangelical believers and churches.

> If association is to be had without amalgamation, then theological education within the independent, evangelical church becomes even more critically important.

Our response is unequivocal in rejecting that kind of post-modern, ecumenical evangelicalism, as well as the more authoritarian brand of fundamentalism that lacks of any desire to demonstrate visible unity among evangelical churches. The danger of spiritual pride is at least as much a problem as the danger of spiritual compromise. Instead, having successfully differentiated what is *distinctive* from what is *essential* to itself, an independent, evangelical church is biblically obligated upon that basis to pursue a more visible demonstration of unity under the Lordship of Christ with those who share essential doctrine. That having been done, then what is needed is to maintain and preserve that which is distinctive. Genuine (dare we say, *biblical?*) ecumenism can only exist where there remain genuine differences.

So the answer to our question is an unambiguous Yes. A church body can and must maintain its theological distinctiveness even while remaining in open fellowship with other evangelicals, and to succeed in that, a church must commit itself to a regular program of theological instruction. People do listen and respond, as demonstrated by the case study described in Appendix A. Incidentally, it simply is not true that contemporary Christians are not interested in doctrine. They are interested in doctrine so long as the instructor is willing to take the time to demonstrate its relevance or applicability to their present-day lives. Theology is not irrelevant or boring, however true that may be of some theology teachers.

In this chapter we have discussed at length the importance of teaching distinctive doctrine in the church. The maintenance of one's theological heritage is a very necessary antecedent to seeking cooperative fellowship with other churches. A broader evangelical union does not necessitate a "least common denominator" form of ministry. In fact, giving attention to theological education within a church will so strengthen its shared conviction over a broad array of subjects as to build confidence in its ability to engage believers from other faith traditions.

Discussion Questions

1. Characterize your own church in terms of how much emphasis it places on the teaching of doctrine. How would you rate your own understanding of doctrine?

2. Describe who Jesus is. How does your view of the Bible (e.g., its authority and trustworthiness) affect your view of Christ?

3. Discuss how your view of Sin (e.g., its source, nature, and extent) helps determine your understanding or appreciation of Christ.

4. Which is worse—the spiritual pride that can attend a strict separatist posture, or the spiritual compromise that may result from a more inclusive stance? Is it possible to guard against either error? How?

5. The author raised the possibility of "genuine," even "biblical" ecumenism. Discuss how a lack of doctrinal homogeneity among churches may actually give rise to greater opportunity for witness in the community.

Chapter 11

The Power to Change

In the last chapter, we looked at how the theological character of a church need not change in order to achieve a degree of inter-church or even intra-church diversity. One can practice a limited, evangelical ecumenism without in the least diminishing one's own theological resolve. Fact is, a healthy spirit of cooperation need not lead a church to discard any of its closely held beliefs. Instead, the varied doctrinal perspectives that each tradition brings to a broad gathering of evangelicals is that which can serve to sharpen one's own apologetic. Some things do not have to change and, more to the point, some things should not change.

That said, some things can change and, indeed, should change. While it is true that adherents to a particular faith tradition should not appear overly anxious to jettison their distinctive beliefs through broader engagement with other Christians, it is at least as true that they should be prepared to hear a good challenge to their views, and even be willing to make some needed corrections to their own theological understanding. On a different but related theme, Christians must be willing to accept correction over any misperceptions they may have concerning the views and perspectives of other participants in the ecumenical enterprise.

But while theological issues are important to consider, in reality these are not the things that normally concern people when faced head-on with the prospect of change. Anxiety over change most often involves lesser things having little or nothing to do with cherished beliefs. Rarely does a church make significant changes to its doctrinal heritage, and that heritage continues to find its way to the pulpit every Sunday morning. The sign out front may read "Evangel Community Church," but discerning individuals know very quickly whether they are part of a Reformed, Wesleyan, or Baptist ministry after just one or two visits. The Pentecostals are even more recognizable. Instead, apprehension over change reaches a high point over the lesser things. Anxiety occurs whenever a change is proposed with respect to music styles, technology upgrades, floral arrangements, and wall paint.

There is very good news on this point, however, for it is precisely in these kinds of areas that people who are accustomed to thinking in terms of "essential" versus "non-essential" are better able to cope with, even welcome, change. Once people have been able to differentiate between what is essential to Christian fellowship of any kind, what is distinctive and therefore nonnegotiable within the limits of one's own church fellowship, and what is heterodox and therefore unwelcome in any church context, they begin to discover that needed change comes more readily and with less anxiety stress. As with many issues in life, with knowledge comes power—in this case, the power to change. Again, that comes as good news, since so many churches need to change in a big way. Let's face it—churches can be downright resistant to change of any kind. In the context of where we've been thus far, perhaps it would be good to consider a few of the reasons why such resistance to change exists within evangelical churches.

Reasons for resistance to change

Throughout church history, change has come slowly for a number of reasons, and not all of them are bad. In fact, the slow pace of change may be given at least partial credit for the degree to which many essential doctrines and practices have been preserved over centuries. Still, an unthinking resistance to change, especially when practiced in the extreme, can be positively stifling to a church's overall health and legitimate growth.

Psychological security. One of the primary reasons for such resistance to change is the feeling of comfort and security that comes with knowing, "here" at least (in church), there is something to grab hold of that is immoveable and unaffected by the dizzy pace of change we observe just outside. To participate in or listen to a Christmas Cantata that sounds just like the one we remembered when we were small gives a sense of stability to an otherwise harried existence. To hear the closing hymn of invitation with which the childhood pastor used to close the service translates into thoughts of "perhaps the world isn't so bad after all." An abiding sense of tradition within the church affords continuity and connectedness with the past, and that leads to good feelings all the way around. This reason for resistance to change is one that is purely psychological. No element of biblical truth is actually put at risk by introducing new worship forms that have no real prescription in Scripture.

Lest anyone misunderstand me at this point, let me hurriedly follow up by saying that tradition is not all bad. Many traditions are very good, especially when they are biblical at their core. For two thousand years, the churches have maintained a tradition of administering baptism and the Lord's Supper. Both of these are very good. More generally, a tradition is beneficial when its purpose for persisting is well understood, and when it is actually fulfilling that purpose. Unfortunately, at least as often as not, traditions tend to stand in the way of an organization's fulfilling its stated purposes.

> A tradition is beneficial when its purpose for persisting is well understood, and when it is actually fulfilling that purpose.

A premium on truth. Another significant reason why people are resistant to change within the church, however, has to do with the fact that church really matters. In other words, we are willing to put up with change in the market place or the entertainment world, because those things are not so important. By contrast, though our checkbooks and busy calendars may suggest otherwise, deep down inside we have an abiding respect for the church. That is because our churches deal in things that we deem to be timeless and changeless—our knowledge of God, the centrality of the Cross, the way of salvation, the hope of resurrection and a better world to come. In other words, church matters because *truth matters.*

Of course, if truth really matters, then most of us presume we must do everything possible to guard it. As it turns out, that is not only a quite reasonable assumption, it is thoroughly biblical (2 Tim 1:14). The problem arises in the methods we then employ to carry out our mandate. The most surefire way of guarding precious truths, we reason, is to guard the forms in which they are presented and proclaimed. We double wrap the bottle to protect the wine inside. We figure that if we do not change the external forms, then we cannot possibly risk changing what is on the inside. But is that a valid assumption?

Unfortunately, countless generations of Christians have found that assumption to be entirely untrue. That is why you can walk into virtually any mainline church and still hear an orthodox expression of belief in the historical reality of Christ, His death and burial, His resurrection, and the life to come. All of that is enshrined in sacred liturgy and sacrament. It matters not whether the congregation and its pastor are theologically liberal, conservative, or something in between. While the words are still there, the meaning behind the words can and do change from place to place. In reality, nothing has been maintained. Instead, everything has been memorialized. Most traditions in churches today are a memorial to the past rather than an effective means of ministry for the present.

In many such churches, the form of worship, the words that are repeated Sunday after Sunday, the hymns that are sung, and any number of lesser traditions, are but a living testament to the day when people actually believed "that stuff." In fact, for those who genuinely seek for a vital and relevant relationship with God through Jesus Christ, the forms which they encounter in such churches that have been unwilling or unable to change may come across as—well, stuffy. Those external forms are viewed as passé, old-fashioned and, worst of all, perhaps even irrelevant. After all, what can a liturgical church caught up in the worship forms of the Middle Ages, or for that matter an evangelical church trapped in a time warp from the 1940's and 1950's, possibly have to contribute to a teenager, young adult, or even a middle-aged adult living in the opening decade of the twenty-first century? The truth is, that church may very well hold the words of eternal life. Unfortunately, most people do not care to stick around along enough to find out, since that church no longer effectively speaks their language.

Fear of the unknown. A third reason for resistance to change is that nobody knows where it will end. If we change "over here," who is to say we won't change "over there" some other time. Who is to say that "the next guy" won't push back a little farther? Again, that is not such a small concern. In fact, it is one that has much validity. There *are* limits to change. Unbridled change can be disastrous to any organization, and it can be downright heretical to a church if done in the wrong manner or if it results in something unbiblical, say, with respect to doctrines or morals. Unfortunately, in response to our fear, we often choose simply to leave everything the same.

The limits of change

So what are the limits of change? This question must be answered before attempting to change anything in the church. We must know what the boundaries are, beyond which no change is permissible. As it turns out, the limits of change, at least for a church, are determined by a couple of criteria that are not the least bit difficult to come up with. I have condensed them under two subject headings. There is the matter of focus, and the matter of faith. Both categories must ultimately deal in what is both essential and distinctive to the church in which change is being contemplated.

No change may alter the biblical focus of a church. Several years ago, I wrote a short booklet entitled *Changing the Mind About Change*. In that booklet, I wrote concerning the little book by Al Ries and Jack Trout called *The 22 Immutable Laws of Marketing*. There the authors lay out a series of "laws" that should govern the way companies adapt themselves and their products or services to a changing marketplace. The book is fun reading, riddled as it is with anecdotal accounts of changes made in corporate America that should never have been made. Often company decision-makers were correct in sensing the need for change, but they proceeded to make changes that hurt instead of helped themselves. As they say, good intentions are not enough. The decision-makers failed to understand the limits of change.

In my booklet on change, I made reference to one such anecdotal account given by Ries and Trout. It concerns a change made at the German auto manufacturing firm BMW, and it serves as an excellent case study. Wanting to shore up sales, BMW decided to change:

> For years, BMW was the ultimate "driving" machine. The company decided to broaden its product-line and chase Mercedes-Benz with large, 700-series sedans. The problem is, how can a living room on wheels be the ultimate driving machine? Not only can you not feel the road, but you'll also crush all the pylons in your driving commercials. As a result, things started downhill for BMW.[1]

In connection with this kind of error in judgment, the authors are stressing (correctly, I believe) that "you become stronger when you reduce the scope of your operations. You can't stand for something if you chase after everything."[2]

As Senior Pastor at Panama Baptist Church, I continue in my attempt to lead our church in a direction that emphasizes the "main thing." A very prominent brochure once stated unequivocally that "Our business is disciple-making." We described how each of our basic ministries contributes to the disciple-making process. Our current brochure says about the same thing, only in a better way. Our mid-week Prayer Bulletins regularly feature requests centered around both personal and corporate evangelism and discipleship. We are making a conscious choice: Our church will be known as a center of discipleship. Period.

That means, quite simply, that any change which can successfully lead us in the direction of more excellent[3] and more effective discipleship is probably a good candidate for acceptance at Panama Baptist Church. Any other kind of change, however noble or novel, that does not either directly or indirectly enable us to do a better job at discipling, is probably a good candidate for rejection. By now we can see how important it is to place limits on the kinds of changes a church is willing to entertain—no change should be allowed to broaden the biblical focus (i.e., mission) of a church. We have already noted how Paul had "become all things to all men so that by all possible means [he] might save some" (1Cor 9:22b).[4] That was his overriding purpose, and the changes he introduced were designed to serve that purpose.

Another way to gauge whether a proposed change may soften the focus of an organization is to run that proposal through the grid of one's core values, assuming that they exist. Panama Baptist Church has eight of them:

- Truth
- Unity
- Compassion
- Community
- Evangelism
- Leadership
- Prayer
- Family

So we ask the question, Does this proposed change guard the truth of our essential beliefs? Does it guard equally well the distinctive beliefs to which we are committed? These kinds of questions are at the top of our list.

Our core values prompt many other questions as well. How will this change affect our people? How will we mitigate those effects? Will this change tend toward division, or will it enhance and strengthen our unity? Will this change attract seekers to our church and to Christ, or will it inadvertently create a barrier to reaching lost people? Will this change encourage and promote the development of our future leadership through apprenticing and mentoring opportunities? How has prayer factored into our decision? Have we sought the Lord's leading through the planning of this change? How have we been able to determine God's answer? How will the change affect our families? Will it give our families more time or less time together?

No change should be made in the absence of faith. Aside from the focus issue, there is the issue of faith. Faithful agents of change do not gamble away existing ministries nor unduly risk the resources that undergird them. In one place, the Apostle Paul wrote about how we are to do "everything," and "everything" includes the desire to make changes: "Everything that does not come from faith is sin" (Rom 14:23). While "faith" can take on different nuances depending on context, here it would appear that there needs to be a settled conviction that what you are about to do is something that God would actually have you to do, and therefore which should succeed, at least as God measures success. Doubtful change, the kind you might enact when you want to try *something* (anything), is not the kind of change that honors the Lord.

What kinds of changes come from faith? There are at least two criteria for making that determination. First, they are the changes that do not contradict the teachings of the church. Within the scope of this consideration are the unambiguous teachings of Scripture. For example, a proposal to introduce a gender-inclusive board of deacons or pastoral staff in order to attract and retain professional women in the church would, in our view, undermine the clear New Testament teaching on this issue.[5] No change should challenge clear biblical principles or precepts, for that would betray a distinct lack of faith in the veracity of God's Word.

Connected with the previous consideration are changes that would directly challenge the distinctive dogmas or doctrinal traditions of a particular church. This is a pragmatic consideration, to be sure, in that attempting to change the teaching standards of a church is bound to introduce unnecessary and destructive division within the assembly. That is true whether or not those standards are the categorical standard of biblical teaching.[6] But because such changes invariably lead to division, this consideration is also a very biblical one: "I appeal to you, brothers, in the name of our Lord Jesus Christ, that all of you agree with one another so that there may be no divisions among you and that you may be perfectly united in mind and thought" (1 Cor 1:10). No change is worth a wholesale congregational meltdown. A change agent who lightly dismisses the possibility of a church split when making plans that involve changes to cherished and distinctive doctrinal standards is in reality dismissing what God has to say on the matter of division. Again, he lacks faith in what God has already spoken.

A second major criterion for determining whether a proposal for change comes from faith is whether that proposal displays a degree of confidence in the outcome. Change in the church ought to be limited by what can reasonably be expected to work. Any proposal for change must be motivated by faith, which is to say there should exist at least a modest expectation that implementing the change will result in a positive outcome. Faith is not about guesswork, nor is it about presuming upon God's ability to override one's own laziness, lack of planning, or failure to research the change proposal. Planning for change in a responsible (faithful) manner will involve giving careful consideration to all potential outcomes and side effects, both positive and negative. Not only must the "good" outweigh the "bad," but the bad has got to be acceptable.

When the United States goes to war, Americans normally understand and anticipate that there will be casualties. The mere possibility of casualties does not in itself render war indefensible. Still, we ask whether the desired outcome or result is of a magnitude to *justify* any casualties. Especially in foreign wars, we justifiably ask what vested interest the United States has in coming to the aid of a foreign power. In more absolute terms, we ask as well how many casualties we can expect to sustain. In the heat of the Cold War, the American drive to keep the Communists out of South Vietnam ended because of an increasing American public perception that keeping South Vietnam free of Communist control could no longer warrant the mounting casualties that were required.[7] There normally is an acceptable level of casualties beyond which a particular goal is no longer worth pursuing.

The same dynamic ought to be present when decisions are made to change in the context of local church ministry. At Panama Baptist Church, we are always asking what changes need to be made to attract more people to one service or another. It is possible that any substantial change will turn some proportion of the existing participants away. The question then largely becomes, do we stand to attract substantially more new participants than we stand to lose. We do not approach that question in a calloused way, but we do recognize that invariably some people will walk away, and often without good reason.

In this chapter, we have looked at the issues of a church's focus and its faith. These categories were meant to begin providing some guidance in deciding where to draw the line on change. When a proposal for change does not adversely affect a church's focus or faith, then it may well be right to begin enacting the change. The list of contrasting labels and descriptors in Table 3 can help characterize a change proposal that you may have. If the change can be characterized as affecting any of the labels or descriptors in the left column, it may be necessary to rethink the proposal.

Table 3. Labels and Descriptors That Characterize Change.

Biblical	vs.	Cultural
Theology	vs.	Taste
Unchangeable	vs.	Changeable
Core Value	vs.	Peripheral
Absolute	vs.	Relative
Principle	vs.	Pragmatism

Discussion Questions

1. List what you and/or your church would consider to be essential doctrine. Explain why these are, or are not, subject to change.

2. List what you and/or your church would consider to be non essential and yet distinctive doctrines. Explain why these are, or are not, subject to change.

3. What kinds of things other than doctrine may be "non-negotiable" in your church? Why?

4. We noted that acting in faith ought to display a degree of confidence in the outcome. Discuss the difference between faith and presumption. Does moving out in faith entail a degree of risk?

5. Can you think of an occasion when you or someone else at church enacted a change that resulted in a marked division within the church? Could that same change have been made in such a way as to avoid division?

Chapter 12

Conclusion

In this book, we have investigated both the ancient Christian creeds and later Protestant confessions in an attempt to establish what previous generations of Christians considered to be the essence of genuine faith. Ultimately and finally, we examined the New Testament and its authoritative, divine witness to what theological commitments constitute "core" or essential Christianity, which is none other than that *kerygmatic*, apostolic proclamation concerning Jesus Christ. The result of this analysis of Scripture, together with the previous investigation of the various creeds and confessions, pointed up the non-negotiable nature of doctrines that centered on the nature of God and the person of Christ (namely, that He is both Lord and Savior), the efficacy of Christ's saving work to rescue us from our sins,[1] the need to appropriate that death by faith, and the necessity of sharing the good news of Christ with lost and sinful people.

The lessening need to separate churches

Having established what is essential to Christian faith, we then set forth several practical applications to the life of the church. Our investigation proceeded on the assumption that what was markedly distinctive about the apostolic proclamation of Christ ought to be what is essential for us. Our first area of inquiry was the extent to which Christians from different faith traditions can cooperate in ministry. We concluded that disagreement over non-essential areas of theological understanding were not so important as to divide equally committed Christians. Distinctive doctrines, while important and deserving of study and articulate defense, are not those things that should automatically discount the possibility of dialogue and collaboration.

That being true, we set out to examine how an independent church might maintain its own distinctive doctrinal commitments, while practicing a sort of evangelical inclusivism in the way it conducts inter-church ministry. We determined that a thoroughly biblical Christian will find unqualified fellowship and cooperation to be possible with anyone who believes that eternal life is found only in the response of faith to God's saving initiative in Christ, a repentant faith in Jesus Christ as Lord and Savior, an owning up to one's own sinfulness and a willful trusting that what God did by Jesus Christ is sufficient to save us. The biblical Christian will work together with those who affirm by word and testimony that these things are true, and he will separate from those professed Christians who do not. Moreover, he will demonstrate charity toward those who disagree with him on secondary theological issues, even as he continues to strengthen his own grasp of various biblical themes and becomes articulate at defending his personal convictions on those themes.

On a closely related subject, in as much as truth is rooted in the authoritative Scriptures, the biblical Christian will demonstrate a willingness to change his views in any area of non-essential belief for which a careful consideration of Scripture has afforded contrary and sufficient evidence, even when that Scripture is mediated by another believer with whom the biblicist may presently disagree. Acceptance of dogma, however historically well-rooted in one's own faith tradition, must always be provisional in nature. It must never be allowed to impede one's personal quest for understanding truth through a study of the source documents themselves, the Holy Scriptures. The Bible must be given freedom to reform and shape one's own theology, however indebted one may be to entrenched church teaching.

The growing need to qualify doctrine

Another point of application has to do with the *place* of doctrine within individual churches. We affirmed without reservation the need to preserve one's doctrinal heritage, while at the same time we observed how every area of doctrine ought not to be placed on an equal footing with every other area of doctrine. There are those teachings that are *essential* to evangelical faith, and there are others teachings that are merely *distinctive* to a particular faith tradition.

In holding fast to both that which is essential and that which is distinctive, balance may be had by adopting some form of doctrinal "taxonomy" whereby a church's theological convictions are presented in a two-tiered hierarchy, the first tier dealing with essential beliefs, the second with distinctive beliefs. Each tier is binding upon a church's constituency to varying degrees, depending on whether an individual is formally outside the church but actively ministering within it (say, a visiting speaker), is included within the church's general membership, or is part of the church's leadership team.

The continuing need to teach doctrine

Another practical outcome of having identified what is "core" to Christian faith relates to the teaching of doctrine. Having laid so much stress upon what is essential, we wanted to follow up by eschewing any notion of settling for a kind of "least common denominator" ministry. Majoring on the essentials need not imply that one avoid the teaching of non-essentials. Instead, each church must remain faithful to Scripture as that body understands it. The fact that some other church disagrees in its reading of any portion of Scripture has no bearing upon what a particular church does with what it "knows." Indeed, it must act upon what it "knows," for whatever is not done in faith is sin (Rom 14:23). If a church is at all faithful to teach the "whole counsel of God," it will continue to define itself theologically by what it purports the Bible to teach.

The evangelical church, accepting the Bible as its sufficient and authoritative canon of truth, must be true to its own understanding of Scripture over a broad range of subjects. As part of its fidelity to that understanding, a church will instill its doctrinal heritage in those affiliated with it. Theological education is a necessary component of responsible ministry. In light of all that has been said concerning the need of believers to visibly display Christian unity, the teaching of doctrine is all the more important for the church which takes its proper place in the wider body of Christ. If church members are encouraged to maintain a healthy openness toward believers affiliated with other faith traditions, they will necessarily come under the influence of teaching in nonessential areas that are opposed to the teaching norms of their own church. If association is to be had without amalgamation, then theological education is of critical importance. Doctrines are lost to a church, not by cooperating with other evangelical churches, but by a failure to teach doctrine.

The power to introduce needed change

Besides a consideration of the *place* of doctrine within the church, we also looked at the beneficial *effect* of doctrine upon the church. Namely, we determined that once people begin to discover that they have been able to differentiate between what is essential versus what is distinctive to their faith, and then having been catechized in that faith, needed change comes more readily and with less stress. When a proposal for change does not adversely affect a church's mission and values, or theological commitments, then it may well be right to begin enacting the change. As with so many issues in life, with knowledge comes power—in this case, the power to change.

Doubtless, much more can be said regarding the place of doctrine in the church. Perhaps others will continue thinking in this area and provide the necessary nuance that may be lacking. This much is clear: The independent church movement must find the courage to examine its use of doctrine in both fellowship and ministry, so that believers may reach their full potential in Christ, that nonbelievers be not hindered in finding salvation through Him, and that God may be exalted through all who together bear His Name. *Soli Deo gloria.*

Discussion Questions

1. Have your personal views on what is essential to Christian faith been adjusted since reading this book? How so?

2. Has this book challenged your views on what are valid reasons for separating from other Christians? How so? How does that affected you?

3. What changes are you planning to make in your own ministry based upon your reading? How will you ensure that those changes are a positive experience for your church?

Appendix A

Teaching Doctrine: A Case Study

—⟋⟍⟍—

Chapter 10 outlined a rather brief defense of the need for theological education in the local church. With that as pretext, the material presented here documents one church's experiment in "comparative theology." The theology is comparative in that it seeks a level of understanding at which people may not only come to understand and appreciate the particular doctrinal views of their own church, but to become discerning enough to be able to identify and differentiate competing theologies when they hear or read them. When I was the pastor of Paw Paw Bible Church, I set out to teach not just a biblical theology through the normal course of Scripture exposition, nor even a systematic theology; rather, I set out to teach an entire theological *system*, and to compare and contrast that system with the more prevalent and competing theological systems that underlie much of the available literature and religious broadcasting that is accessible to church members. Hopefully, the positive result of this experiment may serve as a paradigm for pastors and other church leaders who desire that the flock entrusted to their care receives a strong, theological grounding so that they are free to pursue relationships with individual believers—even churches—that disagree.

The system of theology called Dispensationalism

The system of theology affirmed by the constitution of PPBC (shown in Chapter 9) is known as Dispensationalism. It is important to stress that affirmation as located in the constitution, because prior to teaching a series on Dispensationalism, few in the congregation would have identified that system correctly, in spite of its being there. Even more disturbing, many of those witting enough to understand the formal acceptance of Dispensationalism by PPBC seemed quite willing to give it up, if casual conversation were a valid indi-

175

cator. What people apparently did not understand is that many of their cherished beliefs taken together *are* the unique perspective of a Dispensational viewpoint, especially in the area of eschatology. The need for theological education became clear.

The formal basis of Dispensationalism. Before describing the program by which the members and friends of PPBC were "catechized" in the distinctive Dispensational perspectives of PPBC, we would do well to review exactly what it is we were trying to defend and uphold. A defense of Dispensational eschatology is really a defense of normative "literal," or grammatical-historical hermeneutics. In his book *Dispensationalism*, Charles Ryrie devotes an entire chapter to the question of hermeneutics, in keeping with his *sine qua non* of Dispensationalism.[1] While the material basis of Dispensational teaching is the distinguishing of Israel and the Church,[2] this distinction "grows out of [a] consistent employment of . . . historical-grammatical interpretation." To some minds, the word "literal" denotes the worst sort of unbending allegiance to the wooden meaning of a text. That is not what is meant here. To be sure, in places even Ryrie opts for a more literalistic rendering of a *given* text than other Dispensationalists would be comfortable with,[3] but one should not reject Dispensationalism as a whole on the basis of a selective reading of Ryrie, nor of any other writer for that matter.

More than one critic has charged the Dispensational camp with "run[ning] roughshod over literary genre and interpret[ing] Scripture with a grinding literalism."[4] To be sure, there *are* Dispensationalists who would consistently apply a more stringent brand of "literal" hermeneutic. However, a survey of Dispensationalist literature would reveal that this kind of rank literalism is not the essential bedrock of a Dispensationalist understanding of Scripture. As a group, prominent Dispensationalists (including Ryrie) are able to differentiate between, and are therefore sensitive to, the broad categories of literary genre found in Scripture, such as historical narrative, apocalyptic, and poetry.[5] They are equally comfortable sifting through the various interpretive options afforded by the marked presence within biblical literature of various figures of speech, including such literary devices as metaphor, simile, and hyperbole.

In the end, whether one accepts every interpretive conclusion reached by Ryrie, or any other prominent Dispensationalist writer for that matter, is not the point. The fact remains that Ryrie has correctly identified the hermeneutical system as that which divides evangelical interpreters, whether that system is the consistently literal (historico-grammatical) method of the Dispensationalist; the "theological" and "spiritual" methods of the nondispensationalist/nonpremillennialist (who, according to his view of progressive revelation, allows that the New Testament can, to some degree, change the meaning of the Old), or the more eclectic and mediating "complementary" (already-not yet) hermeneutic of Progressive Dispensationalism.[6]

The material basis of Dispensationalism. Where this consistent literalism most readily plays out may be referred to as the material basis of Dispensationalism. As has already been mentioned, the essence of Dispensationalism is found in its maintenance of a consistent distinction between Israel and the Church, which itself is based upon a consistent usage of the normative grammatical-historical rules of interpretation. This distinction is most readily apparent in the area of eschatology where, based upon a differentiation of Israel and the Church and a literal understanding of the four Jewish covenants (i.e., the Abrahamic, Palestinian, Davidic, and New), a prominent place is reserved for Israel during and following Christ's Second Coming. If nothing else, this method leads to an absolute belief that Christ's return is premillennial, and that the Millennium itself wears a Jewish cast.

The Dispensationalist distinction between Israel and the Church may also be seen in the Dispensational understanding of sanctification. For the Covenant theologian, sanctification is a matter of keeping the Decalogue, which is viewed as still binding today as a rule of life, or divine administration. For the Dispensationalist, the Ten Commandments have passed away as a rule of life, while the "moral law" that informs the decalogue continues under the present administration of grace.[7] The New Testament teaches that "[we] are not under law, but under grace" (Rom 6:14), and that "we serve in the new way of the Spirit, and not in the old way of the written code" (Rom 7:6). By contrast, the Covenantist attempts to resolve the difficulty in his system by dividing the Law into civil, ceremonial, and moral categories, and discarding the first two. While this makes for an attractive solution, it has no basis in Scripture—either the *whole* Law is still in force, or it is not. The New Testament is unambiguous in declaring that it is not.

The point in the foregoing discussion is simply this: there is enough at stake in siding with one or the other theological system that a polemical defense of Dispensationalism within the local church is not only warranted but virtually necessary to the proper maintenance of a shared understanding of Scripture in vital areas of doctrine. The question remains, then, whether this shared understanding of Scripture can be achieved through a comparative study of competing views and reasoned, biblical instruction, or whether that solidarity must come through passive assent to some authoritarian creed. The remainder of this section presents a case study in how one church guided its congregation through a series of deeply theological and polemical lessons on Dispensational eschatology. The material given here emphasizes the eschatological implications of either a Covenantal or Dispensational understanding of Scripture, and argues heavily for the Dispensationalist point of view. The material in this discussion was used as the basis for a series of lessons that were taught at Paw Paw Bible Church in an attempt to strengthen and maintain its Dispensational heritage.

The teaching method at Paw Paw Bible Church

Having briefly described the particular eschatological perspective which PPBC espouses and would desire to preserve for future generations, we can now begin to outline the instructional method that was used at PPBC to win a greater percentage of the congregation to an intelligent acceptance of Dispensational thought, and to objectively measure that result. It cannot be claimed that the method outlined here is the correct one to use because it follows some accepted instructional theory, nor because it has been field tested in a variety of church contexts. Really, its only claim is that it worked in a small to average-sized, independent church. On the other hand, it worked very well, if the pre- and post-survey results can be trusted to any degree. Furthermore, it worked in a church whose average household income and levels of formal education are generally below the national average for evangelical Protestant (read, white-suburban) churches.

The diagnostic questionnaire. To obtain an objective measure of the success or failure of the teaching experiment at Paw Paw Bible Church, we developed a diagnostic questionnaire to ascertain the level of understanding and acceptance of eschatological issues, and their relation to the Dispensational theological system. We asked our people to answer the questionnaire both before and after a lesson series devoted to teaching prophetic themes in the context of a comparative study of various theological systems, including Dispensationalism. The questionnaire is reproduced below:

Prophecy Questionnaire

1) Christ will return to the earth *bodily and physically.*
   - (a) true.
   - (b) false.
   - (c) don't know.

2) As the return of Christ draws nearer in time, the spiritual/ moral climate upon the earth grows
   - (a) worse.
   - (b) better.
   - (c) don't know.

3) Christ's physical rule upon the earth following his return includes a period of time consisting of a thousand years, commonly termed the Millennium.
   - (a) true.
   - (b) false.
   - (c) don't know.

4) Christ will physically rule upon the earth in literal fulfill-ment of Old Testament prophecy.
   - (a) true.
   - (b) false.

(c) don't know.

5) The removal of the church from the earth, commonly called the Rapture, will occur prior to the seven-year period of time known as the Tribulation.
   (a) true.
   (b) false.
   (c) don't know.

6) I consider myself to be a Dispensationalist.
   (a) true.
   (b) false.
   (c) don't know.

7) I consider our statement on Dispensations to be a valuable component of the Paw Paw Bible Church doctrinal statement.
   (a) true.
   (b) false.
   (c) don't know.

The questions are designed to discriminate along several eschatological fronts. For example, the first question concerning the physical and bodily return of Christ establishes whether the individual at least adheres to a generally conservative view of prophetic Scripture.[8] The third question concerning whether Christ's earthly rule includes the millennial period is designed to discriminate the Premillennialist from both the Post- and Amillennialist. The fourth question relating to whether Christ's earthly rule is connected with a literal fulfillment of Old Testament prophecy is key to distinguishing the Covenant Premillennialist from the Dispensational Premillennialist. A complete decision tree suggested by the questionnaire is shown in Figure 4.

The complete set of questions is carefully formulated to demonstrate the importance of Dispensationalism as a theological system to the eschatological position held by PPBC. One purpose in developing the questionnaire and lesson series was in demonstrating that

Figure 4. The Prophetic Decision Tree

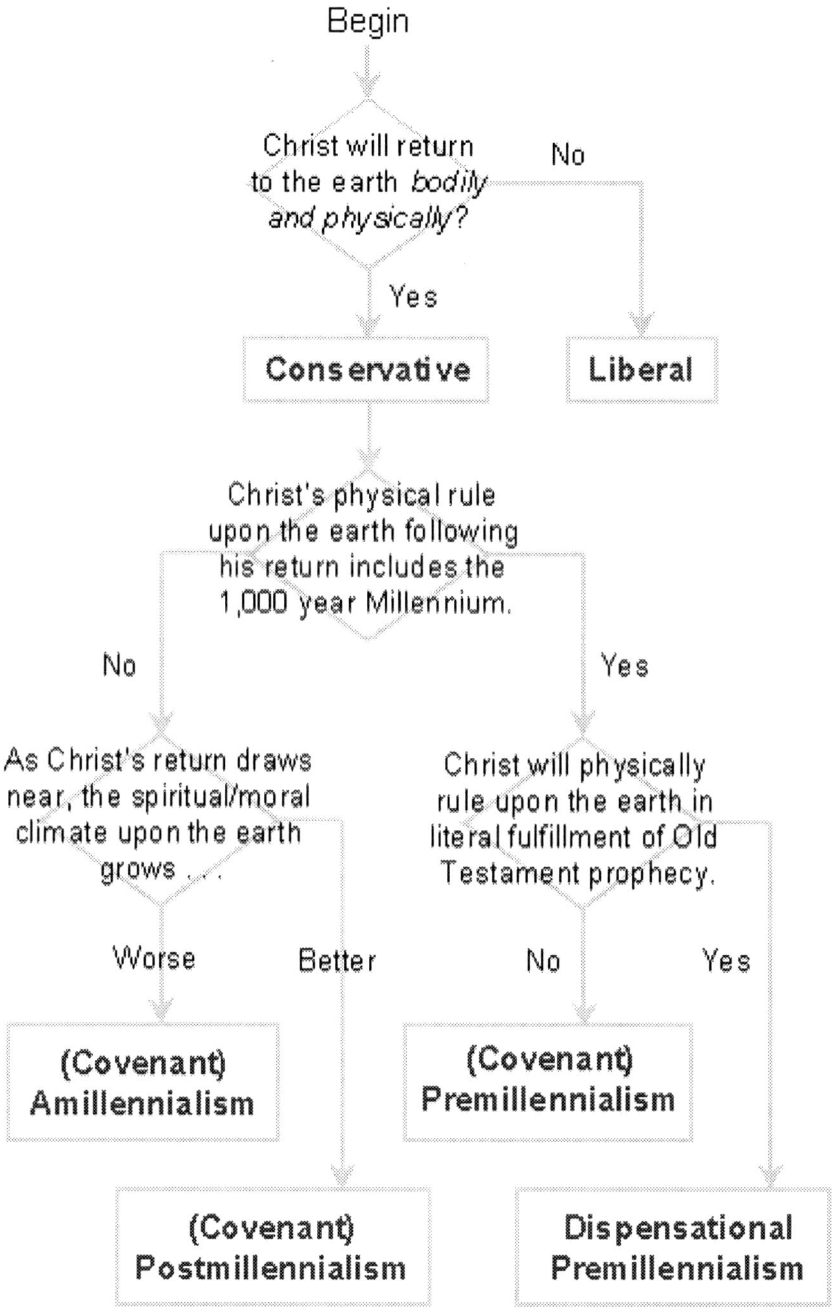

Begin

Christ will return to the earth *bodily and physically?*

No

Yes

Conservative

Liberal

Christ's physical rule upon the earth following his return includes the 1,000 year Millennium.

No

Yes

As Christ's return draws near, the spiritual/moral climate upon the earth grows . . .

Christ will physically rule upon the earth in literal fulfillment of Old Testament prophecy.

Worse

Better

No

Yes

(Covenant) Amillennialism

(Covenant) Premillennialism

(Covenant) Postmillennialism

Dispensational Premillennialism

the eschatological position espoused by the PPBC constitution and generally held by those in the pew *is* precisely the consensus view of Dispensationalism. The fact is, many Christians are Dispensationalists and do not know it, or they hold Dispensational views but have formally disassociated themselves from that theological system because of the degree of criticism being leveled against it by the more mainstream evangelical establishment.[9]

Results of the questionnaire, before and after. Prior to reviewing the results of the pre-instructional survey, an additional comment about the questionnaire would be helpful. Each of the seven questions is designed such that by answering with selection (a), the student is essentially affirming Dispensationalism. In other words, selection (a) is the "correct" answer. By answering with selection (b), the student is denying some tenet of Dispensationalism or, worse yet, orthodoxy in the case of question (1). In the case of questions (6) and (7), the student is devaluing the importance or relevance of maintaining an explicit Dispensational posture. In every question, the selection of (c) indicates that the student did not know the answer or could not answer the question with any confidence.

At the beginning of the lesson series, the entire adult class of 14 responded to the questionnaire. The following table summarizes the students' responses to the questionnaire. Of the 14 students, 10 affixed their names to the question sheet, while four chose to remain anonymous. One rather unscientific way to break down the responses is to consider that, with 14 students answering to seven individual questions, a total of 98 "points" were available to distribute among category (a), (b), and (c) type-responses. Measured this way, 72 points were awarded to category (a), six points to category (b), and 20 points to category (c). In other words, among those who attend Sunday School at PPBC, there was already a fairly good understanding and acceptance of Dispensational, eschatological ideas. The fact that there were only six points given to category (b) responses indicates that there really is not any significant degree of open "hostility" toward orthodoxy, nor toward a Dispensational brand of orthodoxy in particular.

Question Number	Number of (a) Responses	Number of (b) Responses	Number of (c) Responses
1	12	0	2
2	11	1	2
3	10	2	2
4	10	1	3
5	10	1	3
6	10	1	3
7	9	0	5
Totals	72	6	20

The fairly high tally of 20 points against category (c) indicates that there was a definite need to continue with the teaching series, in that several of the participants demonstrated they had little or no understanding with regard to some of the topics being addressed. Two of the students at the beginning of the teaching series were visitors who did not participate in the teaching series. They were unable to attend over several weeks, nor did they retake the questionnaire at the completion of the teaching series. Because our visitors identified themselves on the initial questionnaire, we discounted their contributions to the total point spread, yielding the figures in the table below.

Question Number	Number of (a) Responses	Number of (b) Responses	Number of (c) Responses
1	10	0	2
2	9	1	2
3	8	2	2
4	8	1	3
5	8	1	3
6	8	1	3
7	9	0	3
Totals	60	6	18

In this subset of the data, submitted by the 12 remaining respondents, 60 of 84 responses were favorable category (a) responses, yielding a *71 percent* favorable rating. This score yields a "D+" or "C-" rating for the class, using a typical academic rating scale. At the conclusion of the lesson series, the same questionnaire was administered. At that time, the students were encouraged to answer the questions honestly, that is, according to what *they* understood to be true. They were explicitly cautioned against answering the questions according to how they perceived the instructor may have *wanted* them to respond. The results are shown in the table below.

At the conclusion of the lesson series, 11 respondents turned in 77 individual question responses, of which 75 were favorable category (a) responses, yielding a *97 percent* favorable rating, or an improvement of 26 percentage points over the initial 71 percent score, and earning an "A" or "A+" rating for the class on a typical academic scale. These numbers indicate that the exercise in doctrinal teaching was largely successful, as measured by the results of an objective questionnaire taken before and after the lesson series.

Question Number	Number of (a) Responses	Number of (b) Responses	Number of (c) Responses
1	11	0	0
2	11	0	0
3	11	0	0
4	11	0	0
5	10	0	1
6	10	0	1
7	11	0	0
Totals	75	0	2

Conclusion

We have maintained that independent, evangelical churches that are careful to take their proper place in the wider body of Christ bear a greater responsibility to maintain and promulgate their unique doctrinal perspectives as a hedge against theological amalgamation and compromise. To demonstrate the practicality of teaching theological subjects within the local church, we developed an adult Sunday School lesson series purposely rich in doctrinal content. This series developed some of the finer points of a Dispensational understanding of biblical eschatology, because the need of treating this area of theological study was in evidence at Paw Paw Bible Church, West Virginia, where the author served as pastor.

The adult students who participated in the lesson series were presented with a pre- and post-lesson questionnaire to measure the effectiveness of the lesson series. Our experience with this instructional series showed that a pastor or church leader can "risk" leading his church into more open fellowship with other evangelical groups and churches without suffering doctrinal compromise. He can be effective in ministering the broader theological stance of the church to his flock in such a way that believers are able not only to understand but to *differentiate* that theological stance from competing views. In summary, a church can seek scriptural fellowship on the basis of shared, essential doctrine, while maintaining (even strengthening) what is distinctive about itself.

Appendix B

The GARBC and Cedarville University

—⁓—

—ᴍ—

Figure 5. Cover Letter to the GARBC Council of Eighteen.

Panama Baptist Church

Post Office Box 188   21 North Street   Panama, New York 14767   (716) 782-3035

September 5, 2005

GARBC Council of Eighteen
First Baptist Church
11400 LaGrange Road
Elyria, Ohio 44035-7987

Dear Council:

      I want to thank you for your gracious invitation to address the doctrine of separation and its application to our Fellowship. I have attached a letter that I wrote to one of the leaders within our Empire State Fellowship of Regular Baptists. I believe that it adequately addresses my concerns over recent decisions made by the GARBC with regard to Cedarville University. Currently three of our church's young people attend Cedarville. A fourth student is planning to enroll next year. Our partnership with Cedarville remains strong despite recent actions by the GARBC.

      As my attached letter suggests, our Fellowship has drifted. Whereas the practice of ecclesiastical separation was once a "means to an end," it is now *the end*. There once was a day when we were called upon to separate from Bible-denying infidels so as to preserve orthodoxy within our ranks. Today we are called upon to separate from Bible-believing crusaders for no other reason than to preserve our "separatist heritage." Fact is, we've lost our focus. Our declining numbers and lack of cohesion are all the proof one needs. Please, please, let's get our eyes back on Jesus.

For the Gospel,

Charles J. Colton, Sr. Pastor

Charles J. Colton SENIOR PASTOR   •   Andrew Cook ASSOCIATE PASTOR

189

Figure 6. Letter to the Empire State Fellowship.

Panama Baptist Church

Post Office Box 188   21 North Street   Panama, New York 14767   (716) 782-3035

December 18, 2003

Dear ████:

    Thank you for the helpful information packet concerning the GARBC's partnering arrangement with Cedarville University. By keeping us informed in this way, you do a great service to the churches of our Fellowship. We truly appreciate the effort you have made. We do, however, take issue with a point that you make in Attachment E. For clarity, we quote the passage in question: "[The partnership with Cedarville] sends a wrong signal to the conservatives in the SBC to stay in rather than to be obedient to the Scriptures by leaving the convention and becoming a part of the separatist movement."

    By insisting that Southern Baptist fundamentalists give up their beloved denomination at the very moment they may be winning the war, we surrender a piece of our own thinking during the early years of our struggle in the North. Indeed, we deny a significant part of Regular Baptist history. In a taped interview, Dr. Ketcham remarks, "We had no idea of separation at first, but the longer the controversy raged and *the more hopeless it became to correct it* [emphasis mine], gradually we got the idea that if we can't clean the leaven out of our house, then we must leave the house" (J. Murdoch, *Portrait of Obedience*, p. 110). Quite simply, our separatist "convictions" developed out of a sense of having failed, not from any prior understanding of relevant Scripture.

    Southern Baptists appear to be winning—they are right to "stay in," just as our leaders would have been right to stay in had they been able to turn the liberal tide. Pastor ████ admits as much when he describes recent SBC actions as "truly historic and commendable." The war is not over, but neither is it time to send our SBC brethren any kind of signal that would indicate our disapproval of their efforts. We believe that to act against Cedarville at the present time would do just that. If we would be honest with ourselves, we would readily acknowledge that our reading of certain Scripture passages is colored by our own history—a history which our Southern Baptist brethren do not share. That is why what Cedarville University is doing to encourage our SBC brethren is right, and what the GARBC is proposing by way of response is wrong. And that is one reason why we will continue to commend Cedarville University to our young people.

We remain, together in ministry,

Charles J. Colton, Sr. Pastor   Andy Cook , Assoc. Pastor

Charles J. Colton   SENIOR PASTOR   •   Andrew Cook   ASSOCIATE PASTOR

Notes

—∿∿—

Chapter 1: Introduction

[1] Various Christian denominations baptize either by pouring, sprinkling, or immersion. Eternal Security expresses the view that salvation, once obtained, is forever and can never be lost. Sanctification has to do with the Holy Spirit's work in the life of a Christian to bring his or her life into conformity with the teachings of Christ.

[2] This is the view of postmodernism, for which truth is viewed as being relative and individualistic rather than absolute and universal.

[3] Those holding to a pretribulational Rapture believe that some time in the future, Jesus Christ will return to remove Christians from the earth *prior* to a seven-year period of cataclysmic judgment known as the Tribulation. That is the view held by this writer.

[4] Baptist churches practice this form of church government, stressing the autonomy of each local church, and resisting control by any ecclesiastical hierarchy as represented in the episcopal or presbyterian systems. Within each church, a creative tension normally exists between two opposite but complementary ideas: (1) a subjection on the part of the people to their pastor(s), and (2) a sensitivity on the part of the pastor(s) to the will of the people. See P. Jackson, *The Doctrine and Administration of the Church* (Schaumburg, Illinois: Regular Baptist Press, 1980) 43.

[5] A theist believes in a personal God—one who interacts with and intervenes in history. A deist believes in a God who is distant and uninvolved with history. A pantheist believes in an even less personal God—everything is God and God is everything.

[6] The plural form is intentional, as these groups will not normally associate with one another on account of some difference in theological perspective.

[7] The NAE is shown as essentially occupying ground between the more liberal and fundamentalist wings within Protestantism. It is depicted as stretching back toward Roman Catholicism in view of a concerted move towards rapprochement with Rome by several prominent evangelicals in recent years.

[8] The following extract from a church's constitution is a case in point: "The Church may associate and fellowship with Churches, at any level, which agree with its doctrinal position." In the preceding section, this constitution states that its "missionaries, mission boards, churches and other institutions must indicate *complete* agreement with the Doctrinal Statement" (emphasis mine). The Doctrinal Statement stakes out, among other things, a position on "literal" creationism, a pre-tribulational Rapture, and an explicit theory on the origin of angels.

[9] M. Noll, *The Scandal of the Evangelical Mind* (Grand Rapids: Eerdmans, 1994) 244.

[10] To be sure, some Christian leaders choose to "separate" from representatives of other Christian traditions on purely pragmatic grounds. Still, differences in biblical understanding and practice need not eliminate all forms of cooperative ministry.

Chapter 2: The Historic Creeds and Core Christianity, Part 1

[1] As used in this context, "catholic" refers to the relatively early, visible, professing church that predates even the Roman Catholic Church in its more formal expression. While this catholic church was by no means monolithic and pure in its understanding and practice, still it was much less burdened with the medieval theological and moral "distortions" that gave rise to the Reformation. See T.

C. Oden, *The Rebirth of Orthodoxy* (New York: HarperCollins, 2003) 11.

[2] As context permits, "evangelicalism" in this book is used of that group of Protestant churches and individuals who self-consciously pursue and attempt to practice biblical and apostolic Christian faith, as compared to, say, more contextualized ("de-mytholo-gized") expressions of Christian profession as represented in liberalism and extreme forms of neo-orthodoxy.

[3] Among the Gnostics were those who believed that Jesus' body was phantasmal, or unreal, since all matter was associated with evil (i.e., Docetism), and those who believed that Jesus' body, while real, was merely indwelt by divinity for some period of time (i.e., Cerinthianism). Marcion shared many beliefs with the Gnostics—he believed that Jesus was never born but simply appeared, and that he only seemed to have suffered. See E. Ferguson, "Marcion," *Evangelical Dictionary of Theology* (ed. W. A. Elwell; Grand Rapids: Baker, 1984) 685.

[4] Justification may be defined as that judicial act of God whereby He declares the sinner to be righteous. The basis of justification is the perfect life and atoning death of Christ. The means or condition of justification is faith (Rom 5:1).

[5] The stress upon eternal generation of the Son by the Father does not impair the impressive witness to Christ's Deity within the Nicene Creed.

[6] The so-called "filioque" clause (". . . and the Son"), as added in the West, is retained here. Interesting to our purpose in this book, some issues that divided the Church earlier in its history are hardly mentioned in the creeds and confessions used by fundamentalists today. In fact, the doctrines of eternal generation and procession are increasingly regarded as non-essential to orthodoxy. It would be interesting to know how future generations will regard the many-sided test of orthodoxy currently being used in fundamentalist circles. Dare we question the entrenched insistence upon belief in biblical inerrancy and a literal six-day, recent creation?

[7] A thoroughgoing sacramental view of salvation holds that salvation is transmitted and received through certain symbolic rites of the Church (e.g., baptism) which are considered to be actual

means of grace. The view finds its clearest and most complete expression in the theological perspective of historic Roman Catholicism, which views the sacraments as being effective *ex opere operato* ("from the work done").

[8] Reformation-minded men such as John Wyclif and John Huss had protested Catholic teachings and abuses long before then. Still, it was Luther's movement that began to lead substantial numbers of believers out of the Catholic Church.

[9] An "indulgence" amounted to a reduction in the length of time one had to spend in purgatory. Indulgences were granted upon completion of some special religious deed, such as making a sizeable monetary payment to the Church.

[10] Excerpts presented here were available from http://www.mit.edu/~tb/anglican/intro/39articles.html; Internet; accessed 2 April 2004. Whereas the *Thirty-Nine Articles* (1563) are a moderate and inclusive representation of Reformation theology, they do provide a consistent baseline against which to consider the derivative Anglo-American Baptist and Methodist movements. A more thoroughgoing and classic Reformed statement of belief may be had in both the Second Helvetic Confession (1566), and the Westminster Confession (1647), which briefly governed the Church of England.

[11] Purgatory, in the Roman Catholic and Greek Orthodox view, is a place of temporal punishment that most Christians endure prior to entering into heaven. Evangelicals uniformly reject this doctrine as false and inimical to the Gospel (see Phil 1:23; 2 Cor 5:6-8).

[12] Transubstantiation, in the Roman Catholic view, refers to the manner in which the bread and wine at the Lord's Supper are transformed, as to their substance, into the literal body and blood of Christ, as required by the supposed sacrificial nature of the mass. Evangelicals consider Christ's statements (e.g., "This is my body") as clear examples of direct metaphor, in as much as He was physically present when He made them.

[13] Article III upholds the creedal dogma of Christ's descent into Hell, which Evangelicals accept in differing degrees or not at all. Inclusion of this doctrine in *The Thirty-Nine Articles* does

not detract from an otherwise impressive testimony to the fundamental, historical truths of the Christian faith.

[14] Articles I-V deal for the most part with those subject areas that
are agreed upon by every branch of the western Church, including
Roman Catholicism. It would appear that the Church of England's
stand on Scripture is purposely placed just ahead of those articles
in which it begins to deviate significantly from Catholic teaching,
over such issues as the means of justification and the meaning of
the sacraments.

Chapter 3: The Historic Creeds and Core Christianity, Part 2

[1] Excerpts presented here are taken from E. Hiscox, *The New
Directory for Baptist Churches* (Des Plaines, Illinois: Regular
Baptist Press, 1970) 543-62.

[2] Italicized subheadings have been added to show how clearly that
which is essential to evangelical (Reformed) faith has been distinguished from that which is distinctive to the Baptist tradition.

[3] Together with the *Thirty-Nine Articles*, the *New Hampshire
Confession* deals with God's purpose in Election, although other
Baptist faith statements do not. In connection with the doctrine of
Perseverance, the Reformers taught, properly, that a truly regenerate person will persevere or endure in faith and good works, and
thus be saved to the end. The popular understanding of eternal
security today—that one can believe and be saved forever despite
one's final and utter moral failure—is foreign to Scripture.

[4] It may be interesting for Baptist readers familiar with their own
faith statements to notice the way that more than one emphasis
among Baptists have been lost in practice, if not more deliberately. Article XVII, dealing with the Christian Sabbath, is a case
in point. Those Baptists who have consciously broken with the
Covenanters and aligned themselves with the Dispensationalists
will likely dismiss the concept of a Sunday Sabbath as being
connected with the old economy rather than the new. Similarly,
such Baptists will take a more nuanced approach to Article XIII in
its handling of the Law, and a more expansive approach to Article
XX, fully developing their views of the Rapture and the various

resurrections. The very fact that so many distinctive theological viewpoints have developed only recently should point up the need for permission to differ on secondary issues—even *within* a faith tradition. Among independent Baptists, those who demand uniformity on every point of doctrine would do well to consider that their particular "camp" could not even exist today except that a previous generation of Baptists allowed for meaningful theological reflection within the bounds of scriptural orthodoxy.

[5] Excerpts presented here are from *The Book of Discipline of the United Methodist Church* (Nashville: The United Methodist Publishing House, 1996) 57-63.

[6] *The Book of Discipline*, 50-51.

[7] Article XVIII is a case in point, setting out "only the Name of Jesus Christ, whereby men must be saved." As mentioned already, another example is Article VIII, setting forth the Nicene Creed and Apostles' Creed as that which should be received and believed.

[8] Articles I-IV deal for the most part with those subject areas that are agreed upon by every branch of the western Church, including Roman Catholicism. As was true in *The Thirty-Nine Articles*, Wesley's stand on Scripture is purposely placed just ahead of those articles in which he begins to deviate significantly from Catholic teaching, over such issues as the means of justification and the meaning of the sacraments.

[9] Excerpts presented here were available from http://www. ctsfw. edu/etext/boc/ac; Internet; accessed 22 March 2004.

[10] J. M. Drickamer, "Augsburg Confession," *Evangelical Dictionary of Theology* (ed. W. M. Elwell; Grand Rapids: Baker, 1984) 104.

[11] Ibid., 104.

[12] The Free Church movement is represented historically by groups identified with the Radical Reformation, a diverse movement of Protestant sects (e.g., the Mennonites) which stood in opposition to the state-wed Magisterial Reformation. The Free Church movement is represented in modern times by churches that still evidence a spirit of independence from any external, ecclesiastical authority, such as may be found in America among the loosely-aligned, independent Baptist congregations and "Bible"

churches. My use of the term derives from R. G. Torbct, *A History of the Baptists* (Valley Forge: Judson, 1963) 17.

[13] Article XIII.

[14] At Panama Baptist Church, we maintain that "faith cometh by hearing, and hearing by the Word of God" (Rom 10:17, KJV). Still, when unsaved guests attend our baptismal services, as often they do, we deliberately point to the immersion in water as symbolizing or picturing Christ's death, burial, and resurrection, just ahead of issuing the call to personal faith in Christ as Savior. What is pictured in baptism and the Lord's Supper is consistent with the Gospel proclamation in the Word, and therefore a valid method of witness.

[15] Article IV.

[16] While a sacramental theology is not diametrically opposed to a view of salvation involving grace and faith *per se*, still it tends to promote a works-view of salvation among the laity. Protestant doctrine accords with apostolic teaching: "For it is by grace you have been saved, through faith—and this not from yourselves, it is the gift of God—not by works, so that no one can boast" (Eph 2:8-9).

Chapter 4: Modern Challenges to Core Christianity

[1] J. G. Machen, *Christianity and Liberalism* (Grand Rapids: Eerdmans, 1923) 6.

[2] J. G. Machen, *Christianity and Liberalism*, 7-8.

[3] Preface by R. A. Torrey to *The Fundamentals* (1917; reprint ed.; 4 vols; Grand Rapids: Baker, 1996).

[4] Higher criticism is a form of biblical scholarship that lays stress upon Scripture as literature. Its investigations center upon literary sources and types, and are generally more open to non-traditional views concerning biblical authorship and date of writing. Its practical effect was to undermine confidence in the Bible as Holy Scripture since, in several instances, authorship and date of writing as determined by most critics seemed to challenge that claimed by the biblical text itself.

[5] An affirmation of Scripture, for example, becomes little more than an extended denial of higher criticism.

[6] Inspiration has to do with the idea that the Bible, as well as being the words of men about God, is uniquely the Word of God given to men (2 Tim 3:16; 2 Pet 1:20-21).

[7] As is often the case within reactionary movements, Christian fundamentalism attracted to its leadership ranks a number of strong personalities, among whom there could be little or no shared vision.

[8] G. W. Dollar, *A History of Fundamentalism in America* (Greenville, South Carolina: Bob Jones University Press, 1973) 164. Whereas Dollar acknowledges some of the diseases (i.e., "schisms and bloodletting") that inflict the separatist movement, still he fails to recognize that it is his own brand of militant fundamentalism and the attitude that it breeds which are the primary catalysts for such self-destructive tendencies. Fundamentalists who pride themselves in the "consistency" of their separatism have difficulty knowing when to stop separating. In part, the purpose of this book is to better define the stopping point.

[9] M. Noll, *The Scandal of the Evangelical Mind* (Grand Rapids: Eerdmans, 1994) 243.

[10] G. Marsden, *Understanding Fundamentalism and Evangelicalism* (Grand Rapids: Eerdmans, 1991) 4-5.

[11] G. Wacker, as quoted by G. Marsden, *Understanding Fundamentalism*, 65.

[12] See also, A. McGrath, *Evangelicalism and the Future of Christianity* (Downers Grove: InterVarsity, 1995) 59.

[13] D. A. Carson, *The Gagging of God* (Grand Rapids: Zondervan, 1996) 445.

٨. McGrath, *Evangelicalism*, 57.

McGrath, *Evangelicalism*, 55-56.

Grath, *Evangelicalism*, 66-67.

vard to E. Glenn Wagner, *The Awesome Power of Shared*

ٹs: Word, 1995) vi.

٢r, *The Awesome Power of Shared Beliefs*, 38.

[3] E. Pickering, *Biblical Separation—The Struggle for a Pure Church* (Schaumburg, Illinois: Regular Baptist Press, 1979) 116.

[4] Henry Morris and John Whitcomb, Jr., published *The Genesis Flood* in 1961. In this author's view, his book emboldened many fundamentalists to insist upon uniformity in this area of biblical understanding.

[5] Some fundamentalist Christians revere the King James Version of the Bible as being the sole authoritative translation of the Scriptures available in the English language today. While they differ as to why they use only the King James, the outcome is much the same.

[6] Data through 1990 taken from P. Tassell, *Quest for Faithfulness* (Schaumburg, Illinois: Regular Baptist Press, 1991) 422-23. Subsequent data is from *The World Almanac & Book of Facts* (New York: Newspaper Enterprise Association, Inc).

[7] Quoted in H. Ross, *Creation and Time* (Colorado Springs: NavPress, 1994) 21.

[8] M. Noll, *The Scandal of the Evangelical Mind* (Grand Rapids: Eerdmans, 1994) 189.

[9] Bernard Ramm, for example, drew "friendly" fire with publication of *The Christian View of Science and Scripture* (Grand Rapids: Eerdmans, 1954).

[10] P. Tassell, *Quest for Faithfulness*, 245-47. The resolution affirmed "the immediate creative acts of God" while denying that man derived "from previously existing forms of life," thus denying a place for evolutionary views.

[11] C. I. Scofield, *The Scofield Reference Bible* (New York: Oxford University Press, 1909) 2.

[12] That turns out not to be an entirely static exercise, since the young-earth creationist model itself is evolving. The vapor canopy theory, once popularized by Henry Morris, John Whitcomb, and Joseph Dillow, became an indispensable plank in the young-earth platform, yet it has since been discredited by other more recent young-earth creationist writers. See, for example, K. Ham, et al., *The Revised and Expanded Answers Book* (ed. D. Batten; Green Forest, Arizona: Master Books, 2000) 172-74.

[13] Again, it should be noted that this is entirely consistent with the stated position of the GARBC.

[14] The author's commitment to young-earth creationism has less to do with any conclusion about the literalness of Genesis 1, and more to do with the geological and paleontological implications of a decidedly global deluge in Genesis 6-9.

Chapter 7: Application to Inter-Church Ministry, Part 2

[1] Here we refer to individuals who are equally-committed to the biblical Gospel, and who therefore understand correctly: (1) who Christ is; (2) what He did to save us; and (3) what we must do to be saved.

[2] D. Nettleton, *A Limited Message or a Limited Fellowship* (Schaumburg, Illinois: General Association of Regular Baptist Churches).

[3] J. R. Rice, *Come Out or Stay In* (Nashville: Thomas Nelson, 1974) 182.

[4] J. R. Rice, *Come Out or Stay In*, 179-82.

[5] F. Schaeffer, *The Church at the End of the Twentieth Century* (Wheaton, Illinois: Crossway, 1971) 154.

[6] The "Majority Text" refers to a family of New Testament Greek manuscript copies that predominated the region of Greek-speaking Byzantium following the completion of the New Testament canon.

[7] Secondary separationists are best known for the practice of removing themselves from fellowship with evangelicals who themselves maintain some kind of association with theological liberals, however distant that may be. This gives many independent Baptists, for example, license to exclude all Southern Baptists from cooperative fellowship on the suspicion (likely true) that somewhere a liberal is "ministering" under Southern Baptist sponsorship. The GARBC recently ended its formal partnership with Cedarville University just because that institution had entered into an informal but public partnership with the Southern Baptists of Ohio. According to John R. Rice, writing in the mid-1970's, even separatist Bob Jones University had

Southern Baptists on its governing board. See J. R. Rice, *Come Out or Stay In*, 214. See Appendix B for the author's correspondence related to the Cedarville decision.

[8] One need only to read the minutes of meetings and the informal histories of many of the older, established Baptist churches to see that this is true. A fundamentalist prophetic conference held at New York City in 1878, together with a follow-up conference at Chicago in 1886, featured Baptist, Presbyterian, Methodist, Congregational, Lutheran, and Reformed Episcopalian speakers. See G. W. Dollar, *A History of Fundamentalism in America* (Greenville, South Carolina: Bob Jones University Press, 1973) 28-41, 43-45. Dollar, himself a "militant" fundamentalist, describes the 1878 gathering as "the first important conference of Fundamentalism." He refers to the 1886 conference as a "Plymouth Rock in the history of Fundamentalism" and a "Magna Charta of its doctrinal insights."

[9] According to George, a refusal to allow diversity results in an "artificial oneness." See T. George, "Is Christ Divided?" *Christianity Today* 49 (July, 2005) 33.

[10] Perhaps that was more true in the early part of the twentieth century. Presently, it is the liberal who tolerates the minority presence of evangelicals.

[11] The controversy is baseless as a test of fellowship. It is perfectly valid to maintain a preference for a certain family of biblical manuscripts, or even for a particular translation. The problem arises when the results of extra-biblical (not arising from the text of Scripture itself) scholarship or personal preference is made the pretext for separation.

[12] C. R. Swindoll, *The Grace Awakening* (Dallas: Word, 1996) 194.

Chapter 8: A Practical Guide to Cooperative Ministry

[1] Julia's Restaurant recently closed. It was located on the "four-corners," as they call most intersections around here.

[2] "Liturgical" is codeword for "Lutheran" in southwestern New York.

[3] Article IV deals, among other things, with the particular views of PBC on eternal security, spiritual gifts, the Rapture, and various other Baptist distinctives. Doctrinal views are purposely presented in two sections, the reasons for which are discussed in the next chapter.

[4] B. Graham, *Just As I Am* (New York: HarperCollins, 1997) 129.

[5] B. Graham, *Just As I Am*, 303-04. In response to his developing ecumenism, Graham was to receive pointed criticism from leading fundamentalists, among them Bob Jones, Carl McIntire, and John R. Rice.

[6] F. Schaeffer, *The Church at the End of the Twentieth Century* (Wheaton, Illinois: Crossway, 1971) 143.

[7] G. W. Dollar, *A History of Fundamentalism in America* (Greenville, South Carolina: Bob Jones University Press, 1973) 279-80.

[8] J. R. Rice, *Come Out Or Stay In* (Nashville: Thomas Nelson, 1974) 215.

[9] J. R. Rice, *Come out Or Stay In*, 227.

[10] F. Schaeffer, *The Church at the End of the Twentieth Century*, 151.

[11] F. Schaeffer, *The Church at the End of the Twentieth Century*, 158.

Chapter 9: Application to Intra-Church Ministry

[1] A good example might be where teachers are required to review and sign a doctrinal statement on some periodic basis.

[2] In the view of some fundamentalists, "teachable" means "a willingness to subscribe to distinctive doctrines given enough time." The author attended an independent church outside Boston during college. After he had sat under the church's teaching for a few years without adopting their KJV-only position, he was directly confronted by a member of the church regarding the certainty that he had never been truly saved. Needless to say, he was not a viable candidate for membership.

[3] Historically, many Baptists have stressed a view of original sin which teaches that a sin nature (a natural propensity toward sin) is transmitted in hereditary fashion from generation to generation,

beginning with Adam. Theologians in the Reformed tradition do not disagree, but they speak as well of some type of "immediate" imputation of Adam's sin to the human race. Baptist theologian Emery Bancroft makes no mention of imputed sin in his treatment of this subject. See E. Bancroft, *Christian Theology* (Grand Rapids: Zondervan, 1976) 212-13. For a concise discussion of the development of the Reformed view of original sin, see L. Berkhof, *Systematic Theology* (Grand Rapids: Eerdmans, 1941) 237-39.

[4] The stress upon one's present "possession" does not add works to grace. A true conversion experience, involving genuine repentance from sin and faith in Christ, results in a salvation that is "worked out" in life, as God works in us "to will and to act according to his good purpose" (Phil 2:12-13). Every professing Christian is called upon to "make [his] calling and election sure" (2 Pet 1:10).

[5] Baptists have insisted upon immersion as the acceptable mode of baptism because, among other things, it is the only method that properly depicts the death, burial, and resurrection of Christ (Rom 6:4).

[6] Among other things, that means we "safeguard the unity of our church by conforming to its doctrines and practices."

[7] D. Wallace, *Crisis of the Word*; on the Internet at http://www.bible.org/page.asp?page_id=705; accessed 16 August 2005. Wallace lends his authoritative voice to a rising chorus of voices within fundamentalism that is asking related questions and issuing similar proposals. See Chapter 4 for D. A. Carson's concern that the formal principle of belief in the "truth, authority, and finality" of the Bible be at the center, as well.

Chapter 10: The Importance of Continued Indoctrination

[1] T. C. Oden, "Why We Believe in Heresy," *Christianity Today* 40 (March 4, 1996) 12.

[2] T. C. Oden, *The Rebirth of Orthodoxy* (New York: HarperCollins, 2003) 131.

[3] In 1921, liberals within the Northern Baptist Convention understood this all too well. Fundamentalists had called for the adoption of an explicit statement of faith. Liberals proceeded to replace that motion with one calling for adherence to the "New Testament" as the sole rule of faith and practice. This move left the field of biblical interpretation wide open. See G. W. Dollar, *A History of Fundamentalism in America* (Greenville, South Carolina: Bob Jones University Press, 1973) 155.

[4] A. Hoekema, *The Four Major Cults* (Grand Rapids: Eerdmans, 1963) 53-54.

[5] B. Graham, *Just As I Am* (New York: HarperCollins, 1997) 559.

[6] Preaching to the felt needs of a congregation is a legitimate way to arrest attention and make forceful application. Along the way, however, the faithful preacher will bring his theology of sin, salvation, and sanctification into the proposed solution.

[7] That, indeed, is the first step in theological education — getting the layperson to see the benefit in being grounded theologically. In the end, the Christian's ability to function well in life is based more in understanding and apprehending the unchanging character of God, and less so in his grasp of multi-step solutions to life's many pointed problems.

[8] Dominion Theology, as espoused by the Reconstructionist Presbyterians who are post-millennial in their eschatology, calls upon Christians to bring all societal institutions under the theocratic rule of God in necessary preparation for the coming of Christ.

Chapter 11: The Power to Change

[1] A. Ries and J. Trout, *The 22 Immutable Laws of Marketing* (New York: HarperCollins, 1993) 32-22.

[2] Ries and Trout, *The 22 Immutable Laws*, 31.

[3] "Whatever you do, work at it with all your heart, as working for the Lord. . . . It is the Lord Christ you are serving" (Col 3:23-24).

[4] In connection with the subject matter of this section, we should point out that the initial salvation experience (conversion) is only the beginning of what it means to be saved. Biblical salvation

is better understood as being a past, present, and future reality. Some theologians refer to these three components as positional, progressive, and perfective sanctification (or, even better, justification, sanctification, and glorification). Of the three, the first two components normally require the active participation of one or more disciplers in the context of a church-based ministry of discipleship.

[5] This becomes clear when the relevant biblical passages (e.g., 1 Cor 11:3; 1 Tim 2:12-13; 1 Tim 3:8-12) are carefully considered in their historical and grammatical contexts. See, for example, the careful exegesis and commentary on 1 Tim 2:8-15 in W. Mounce, "Pastoral Epistles." *Word Biblical Commentary* (ed. B. Metzger; 53 vols.; Nashville: Nelson, 2000) 46:105-147.

[6] Here we are not talking about essential Christian doctrine such as that concerning the Person of Christ, His atoning death and resurrection, or how all of that is applied to individuals for salvation. We are referring to those multiplied issues over which equally-committed Christians may disagree.

[7] This undoubtedly is a one-sided and uncritical perspective on the events surrounding the American involvement in Vietnam, but hopefully the illustration is helpful to the present discussion.

Chapter 12: Conclusion

[1] Christ's salvific work absolutely centers on His vicarious death (1 Cor 2:2), however that death depends for its validity and efficiency upon His bodily resurrection, without which Christ is not validated as to His Person, and sin and death are not vanquished.

Appendix A: Teaching Doctrine: A Case Study

[1] Dispensationalists can be credited with renewing a healthy interest in hermeneutics during recent years. Biblical *interpretation* had been given little attention due to the greater controversy surrounding biblical *inerrancy*. Walter C. Kaiser, Jr. made the astute observation that "a strong confessional stand on Scripture and its inerrancy could remain orthodox, even long after the prac-

tice and method of interpreting Scripture had turned neoorthodox or liberal" [W. Kaiser, "Legitimate Hermeneutics," *Inerrancy* (ed. N. Geisler; Grand Rapids: Zondervan, 1980) 147]. Interpretation becomes all the more critical when it is understood that virtually *anyone* may claim to be an inerrantist, so long as that word is carefully nuanced.

2 C. Ryrie, *Dispensationalism* (Chicago: Moody, 1995) 41. The necessity of maintaining a clear distinction between Israel and the Church is apparently the first among equals in Ryrie's list of three essentials.

3 For example, Ryrie concludes (or at least *strongly* infers) that horses and chariots, bows and arrows, shields and helmets, clubs, swords, and spears *must* be the literal weapons of choice when a northern confederacy attacks Israel (Ez 38-39), presumably during the first half of the Tribulation. See Ryrie, *Dispensationalism*, 82.

4 B. Ramm, *Protestant Biblical Interpretation* (Grand Rapids: Baker, 1970) 146.

5 Walvoord, for example, devotes several introductory pages of his commentary on Revelation to a discussion of the rich symbolism in that book because of its apocalyptic character. He writes of how apocalyptic books "reveal truth expressed in symbolic *and guarded* language" [emphasis mine], and concedes that "there will never be complete agreement on the line between imagery and the literal." See J. Walvoord, *The Revelation of Jesus Christ* (Chicago: Moody, 1966) 26, 27-28.

6 For an authoritative survey of Progressive Dispensational ideas, see C. A. Blaising and D. L. Bock, *Progressive Dispensationalism* (Wheaton: Victor, 1993).

7 See the discussion in R. Lightner, "Covenantism and Dispensationalism," *The Journal of Ministry and Theology* 3:2 (Clarks Summit, Pennsylvania: Baptist Bible Seminary, 1999) 71-74. See also A. G. Fruchtenbaum, *Israelology: The Missing Link in Systematic Theology* (Tustin, California: Ariel Ministries, 1989) 643ff.

8 Millard Erickson notes that "conservatives reached a consensus on the major points of eschatology by the beginning of the twen-

tieth century." Among the issues he includes in that consensus—
"At some future time Christ will return bodily and personally."
See M. Erickson, *A Basic Guide to Eschatology* (Grand Rapids:
Baker, 1998) 12.

[9] For example, Mark Noll equates Dispensationalism with "simple
anti-intellectualism" and "intellectual sterility." See M. Noll,
The Scandal of the Evangelical Mind (Grand Rapids: Eerdmans,
1994) 123, 137.

Bibliography

—ⱴⱴ—

Bancroft, E. *Christian Theology.* Grand Rapids: Zondervan, 1976.

Berkhof, L. *Systematic Theology.* Grand Rapids: Eerdmans, 1941.

Blaising, C. A. and Bock, D. L. *Progressive Dispensationalism.* Wheaton: Victor, 1993.

Carson, D. A. *The Gagging of God.* Grand Rapids: Zondervan, 1996.

Colton, C. *Changing the Mind About Change.* Panama, New York: Panama Baptist Press, 2002.

Dollar, G. W. *A History of Fundamentalism in America.* Greenville, South Carolina: Bob Jones University Press, 1973.

Drickamer, J. M. "Augsburg Confession." *Evangelical Dictionary of Theology.* Ed. W. M. Elwell. Grand Rapids: Baker, 1984.

Erickson, M. *A Basic Guide to Eschatology.* Grand Rapids: Baker, 1998.

Fee, G. *The First Epistle to the Corinthians.* NICNT. Grand Rapids: Eerdmans, 1987.

Ferguson, E. "Marcion," *Evangelical Dictionary of Theology*. Ed. W. M. Elwell. Grand Rapids: Baker, 1984.

Fruchtenbaum, A. G. *Israelology: The Missing Link in Systematic Theology*. Tustin, California: Ariel Ministries, 1989.

George, T. "Is Christ Divided?" *Christianity Today* 49 (July, 2005) 31-33.

Graham, B. *Just As I Am*. New York: HarperCollins, 1997.

Ham, K., et al. *The Revised and Expanded Answers Book*. Ed. D. Batten. Green Forest, Arizona: Master Books, 2000.

Hiscox, E. *The New Directory for Baptist Churches*. Des Plaines, Illinois: Regular Baptist Press, 1970.

Hoekema, A. *The Four Major Cults*. Grand Rapids: Eerdmans, 1963.

Jackson, P. *The Doctrine and Administration of the Church*. Schaumburg, Illinois: Regular Baptist Press, 1980.

Kaiser, W. "Legitimate Hermeneutics." *Inerrancy*. Ed. N. Geisler. Grand Rapids: Zondervan, 1980.

Lightner, R. "Covenantism and Dispensationalism." *The Journal of Ministry and Theology* 3:2. Clarks Summit, Pennsylvania: Baptist Bible Seminary, 1999.

Machen, J. G. *Christianity and Liberalism*. Grand Rapids: Eerdmans, 1923.

Mare, W. H. "1 Corinthians." *The Expositor's Bible Commentary* Ed. F. Gaebelein. 12 vols.; Grand Rapids: Zondervan, 1976.

Marsden, G. *Understanding Fundamentalism and Evangelicalism.* Grand Rapids: Eerdmans, 1991.

McGrath, A. *Evangelicalism and the Future of Christianity.* Downers Grove: InterVarsity, 1995.

Morris, H. M. and Whitcomb, J. C. *The Genesis Flood.* Philadelphia: Presbyterian and Reformed, 1966.

Mounce, W. "Pastoral Epistles." *Word Biblical Commentary.* Ed. B. Metzger. 53 vols. Nashville: Nelson, 2000.

Murdoch, J. M. *Portrait of Obedience.* Schaumburg, Illinois: Regular Baptist Press, 1979.

Nettleton, D. *A Limited Message or a Limited Fellowship.* Schaumburg, Illinois: General Association of Regular Baptist Churches.

Noll, M. *The Scandal of the Evangelical Mind.* Grand Rapids: Eerdmans, 1994.

Oden, T. C. *The Rebirth of Orthodoxy.* New York: Harper-Collins, 2003.

_____. "Why We Believe in Heresy." *Christianity Today* 40 (March 4, 1996) 12-13.

Pickering, E. *Biblical Separation—The Struggle for a Pure Church.* Schaumburg, Illinois: Regular Baptist Press, 1979.

Quebedeaux, R. *The Worldly Evangelicals.* New York: Harper & Row, 1978.

Ramm, B. *Protestant Biblical Interpretation.* Grand Rapids: Baker, 1970.

_____. *The Christian View of Science and Scripture*. Grand Rapids: Eerdmans, 1954.

Rice, J. R. *Come Out or Stay In*. Nashville: Thomas Nelson, 1974.

Ries, A. and Trout, J. *The 22 Immutable Laws of Marketing*. New York: HarperCollins, 1993.

Robertson, A. T. *The Epistles of Paul*. Word Pictures in the New Testament. Nashville: Broadman, 1931.

Ross, H. *Creation and Time*. Colorado Springs: NavPress, 1994.

Ryrie, C. *Dispensationalism*. Chicago: Moody, 1995.

Schaeffer, F. *The Church at the End of the Twentieth Century*. Wheaton, Illinois: Crossway, 1971.

Scofield, C. I. *The Scofield Reference Bible*. New York: Oxford University Press, 1909.

Swindoll, C. R., *The Grace Awakening*. Dallas: Word, 1996

Tassell, P. *Quest for Faithfulness*. Schaumburg, Illinois: Regular Baptist Press, 1991.

The Book of Discipline of the United Methodist Church. Nashville: The United Methodist Publishing House, 1996.

The Constitution of the Paw Paw Bible Church. Paw Paw, West Virginia: Paw Paw Bible Church, 1998.

The World Almanac & Book of Facts. New York: Newspaper Enterprise Association, Inc., 1995, 2000.

Torbet, R. G. *A History of the Baptists*. Valley Forge: Judson, 1963.

Torrey, R. A. Preface to *The Fundamentals*. Reprint ed. 4 vols. Grand Rapids: Baker, 1996.

Wagner, E. G. *The Awesome Power of Shared Beliefs*. Dallas: Word, 1995.

Wallace, D. *Crisis of the Word*. On the Internet at http://www. bible. org/page. asp?page_id=705. Accessed 16 August 2005.

Walvoord, J. *The Revelation of Jesus Christ*. Chicago: Moody, 1966.

How To Become A Christian

—∿—

ADMIT... that you are a sinner and want to be cleansed from your sin. You cannot save yourself no matter how good you may be, or how hard you may try.

"For all have sinned and fall short of the glory of God" (Rom 3:23).

BELIEVE... that God loves you and sent His Son, the Lord Jesus, to die on the cross to pay for your sins. Believe that He came alive again, overcoming sin and death.

"But God demonstrates his own love for us in this: While we were still sinners, Christ died for us" (Rom 5:8).

CALL... upon the Lord, asking Him to save you. Confess your sin to Him. Tell Him that you want to be saved from the power and penalty of sin. Tell Him that from now on you are trusting *Jesus* alone to save you from your sins.

"For everyone who calls on the name of the Lord will be saved" (Rom 10:13).

Printed in the United States
203334BV00005B/286-303/A

9 781600 343490